SELECTED POEMS

ARTHUR SALE

Selected Poems

Arthur Sale

with a Foreword by Helen Vendler

The Pentland Press Ltd
Edinburgh · Cambridge · Durham · USA

© Arthur Sale 1999

First published in 1999 by
The Pentland Press Ltd.
1 Hutton Close
South Church
Bishop Auckland
Durham

British Library Cataloguing in Publication Data.
A catalogue record for this book is available
from the British Library.

ISBN 1 85821 650 8

Typeset by George Wishart & Associates, Whitley Bay.
Printed and bound by Bookcraft Ltd., Bath.

Contents

Foreword

Arthur Sale's volume contains two long poems and some shorter ones, and anyone reading it will be won, first and foremost, by the two long sequences. The first, *The Willow*, is about a natural object – the willow tree in the poet's front garden; the second, *The Bridge* is about a man-made work – the bridge at Clare College, Cambridge. Both tell of a succession of encounters with the object over time: both exemplify the power of the poetic mind, as it pours itself into a non-human thing, to invest that thing with aura, value, and presence.

I can testify to that power; I could never look at the Clare Bridge again in the same way after reading Sale's meditations on it; and every willow tree I see (at least any possessing the majesty described by the poet) is now Sale's willow. As Elizabeth Bishop said in a 1962 letter to Robert Lowell, "If, after I read a poem, the world looks like that poem for twenty-four hours or so, I am sure it's a good one – and the same goes for paintings. I studied a huge book on Bosch for several days – and the world looked like Bosches for a month afterwards." A true poem makes the reader see the world, for some time, as the poet saw it. Sale's poems exert that afterpower.

Let me, as a reader familiar with them, give a brief account of what happens in the first of these marvellous sequences. Then let me comment on the second of them, and add a word about the Sale style – its attractions, its difficulties, its reason for being. But – to begin with – *The Willow*.

In the paradoxically-named "Prelude Postscript," we see the identification of the author (Sale) with the willow (*Salix* is its Latin name), whom he addresses as "Dear enemy" because it is gradually taking over his garden, usurping the root-room of the former silver birch, elm, and ash. The poem is a hymn to trees in general (in which the ancient California redwoods come in for special mention): why, the poet asks, should the willow be an Attila to its own genus?

The next lyric, "Down by The Sally Gardens," begins as a series of instructions for anyone attempting, skirting the willow, to reach Sale's front door; it then recapitulates the history of the poet's willow. The tree was planted on V-Day, and is now reaching its "silver anniversary". It has consumed all the nearby trees; surely it now aims for the house? The poet utters an ironic plea: "Do not ingest us," and compares the unnervingly rapid growth of his willow to the slow millennial growth of bristle-cone pines in California, where a seven-hundred year old tree is still a "stripling", and the pine's full height is reached only after four thousand years.

"Two Way Sees Through" contrasts art and nature, as the poet compares the way sunlight comes in unimpeded at his office – where he sits, preoccupied with art, the sun silhouetting his head and book on the wall – with the way the sunlight comes in through his window at home, where the willow's branches constantly make and unweave their crossings ("like / the building China Wall three steps and back"). The willow itself is compared to a palace, with "queen post galleries and stairs" in which the light is constantly being freshened into those "central azures" which are "pictures blank / to feed our feelings fullest beyond art."

The sequence continues with "Willow Stay Bare," a meditation on the dual nature (beautiful and predatory) of the tree, and on its eventual mortality. The willow has destroyed (by its roots) the spring bulbs from which the poet expected flowers; and the roots have even penetrated the drainpipes of the house. Yet the poet cannot deny the willow's beauty; he sees the tree now as a sculpture (better than the crisscrossed wire constructions of Naum Gabo); it is a "blueprint of space", yet also the world-tree Yggdrasil; it is a ziggurat, an igloo cathedral. It is inhabited by a world of birds, by the squirrel, the cat – a whole ecology, like a termite mound. Or it is the green glowing Hades of the medieval Sir Orfeo; or, as it rustles in the wind, it is the fabled allegorical Rumour full of tongues. The poet imagines the willow's ultimate death – Armageddon or Götterdämmerung— but ends hailing the image of the tree as one inexhaustible to sight, "a re-/velation like a throbbing galaxy / to tax the reverent the revelling eyes."

"Sing All A Green Willow Must Be My Garland" is a two-part poem, covering winter and spring: *Winter Greens* asserts that even though wind and rain have damaged the willow, it can still "hatch and hutch a marvel" with its "golden utterance of a green outlaw thought." And in *Verdigris*, the spring moss that illuminates the limbs of the willow illustrates the alchemy of renewal: the tree remains equable, whether in the face of outside provocation – "aggro trouble on invaded pitches by mufflered fans" – or upstart young "procreant cradles endlessly rocking."

"Not Proven Or Still O The Will O" addresses the difficulty of making art in the present time: though the poet composes himself ("the die is cast") to write, the poem delays. His "filibuster preface" spreads itself out into a redescription of the tree. While he waits, the poet is reminded of Beckett's minimal but driven drama of the single speaking Mouth, and of the screams painted by Munch and Bacon, which signify "the now impossibility of art / to become art for its or any sake."

The willow's limbs have been lopped: in "No Numbers Please," it is now "tree basic minimal abstract of tree." Though the poet's house has been saved from the threat of "deadly piping roots", he regrets the absent, "negative", limbs, but foresees the willow's spring rehabilitation. For the moment, a lopped limb of the willow is placed upright on his hearth, a Tom Thumb reminiscent of "that gaunt gianthood its source."

The willow is now, by the time "Absalom My Son Absalom" is composed, a half-century old. To the poet's wife it seems a third son ("born" between his two natural sons) or perhaps a "desired daughter" – but in these days of unisex long hair, one can hardly decide. However, its growth, marking danger to the house, means that it has to be pruned almost mortally – "denuded / defrocked and not quite drawn and quartered." The poet continues Marvell's reflection, "So carpenters do square and hew / Green trees that in the forest grew," asking "what cruelty or necessity" in life requires the shearing plane as it smooths the plank, or the glacier that smooths out rocks. (In a comic moment, the poet reflects that his balding elder son has been denuded of his hair too, but his loss, unlike the willow's, is permanent.) The poet then remembers another son, the Biblical one hanged by the hair, Absalom. "Family divergences" are obliquely recalled, but by the end, sons and tree alike still stand.

The coterminous life and expected death, of the poet and his tree generate "Final Demand." A large limb of the willow has fallen in a storm, intimating decay within. The poem becomes a hymn to the tree, declaring that the poet has never seen it as a threat but rather as "a bean stalk world of wonder" to which the poet's eye has been "poor Jack," "privileged to wander . . . at will" the radiant arteries of the tree, its "oriels and oubliettes and Mars canals." But "this dropped portcullis" of the fallen limb "reveals a new dimension of intent," a "bamboo bombing" that presages, "given our nearness a destined some time end / to both," a death, the poet says, assenting, "you cannot desire much worse than I."

"Towards Amends" offers an apology to the tree, ending in an intense communion with it (and with the natural universe that it represents). "Even though I have named you by fantastic names," says the poet (recapitulating those names), "do not / answer me in that same despiteful kind," but rather bend on me your "concentrated presence . . . collected from root bole branch grounded hair,"

> impenetrable to question and the need
> to sentence or forgive unthinkable –
> and I am answered though no longer there.

In the last line, the poet disappears, and the tree has become the universe itself, an impersonal universe which cannot be questioned, which has no need to sentence or to forgive its inhabitants, but whose presence alone suffices the grateful consciousness that has encountered it

And finally, in the epilogue, "Willow Pattern," the poet offers a reprise of his two central images – willow and bridge, nature and art – as they are united by his wife, whose Coleridgean "esemplastic vision . . . envelops them within a harmony."

*   *   *

I have given this brief summary of the poet's exchanges with the willow because a reader may not at the outset be at home in Sale's stream-of-consciousness. Yet the surface of the poem is attractive enough to draw a new reader in, precisely because of the poet's eddies and flashes of charged language. "A poem," said Wallace Stevens, "must resist the intelligence almost successfully." It is the "almost" on which the poet counts; the reader must sense the resistance of idiosyncratic language, while feeling as well the presence of the clue-thread in the hand that will lead him both into and out of the labyrinth.

In each one of Sale's poems that thread is vividly felt, while equally, in every one, the style suggests a complex mind, rich in both cultural and natural knowledge, bringing itself fully to bear on both

x

the outside world and its own mixed responses to that world. The poems are testimony not only to the powers of consciousness (that can derive so much, for instance, from a single tree or a single bridge), but also to the powers of affection maintained over many years. Sale's genres are the genres of affection – the hymn, the elegy, the colloquy. The poems naturally, then, sequester themselves in the sites of affection, the brain and the heart, and they speak in the languages of both: in free association and private reference, intimate address and meditative passion. These inner monologues are accompanied by rueful backward glances and forward fearfulness, as seasons change and years pass. We watch the poet's art "conspiring" (to use Keats's term) with the willow and the bridge to construct that rare third thing, a moving trace of the aesthetic consciousness as, by devotion, it unites itself to an object.

"The bridge is always moving," says the opening line of Sale's second poetic sequence, because the mind contemplating the Clare Bridge (with its three arches surmounted by a symmetrical series of stone balls) is itself always moving. The bridge is a solace to the poet (in this poem begun in "a world washed flat by total war"). As the poet addresses the bridge (with its "curved incumbent curbs," its "semicircles", "all aspirations to the perfect orbs / poised on your bevelled ledge"), it takes on allegorical weight:

> compere to the past but not dry as dust,
> eloquent now and despite boasting steel
> still
> a working model and a gracious thrust
> to the future – if we can cease to kill.

The bridge has been "restored", but one cannot by restoration put the clock back. Nor can one restore the world we had before the atom was split – and Sale's poem is one of the first to record the intellectual and moral impact of that unprecedented explosion, when

> the approved indefinitely ductile
> ligaments of the body of the dance,
> beyond earthlong endurance elongated
> by a fanatical new dancing master,
> snapped.

A winter flood submerges the bridge: "I saw / you sunk and fighting white-gilled for your life," says the poet, and, worse yet, he perceives that the bridge is not wholly symmetrical: "the last arch's outmost pier is not / flexibly free, as I had dreamed." Yet why should the bridge be less flawed than he? "I was / an antipodean casualty, you know, of Nagasaki and Hiroshima." It is the permanence and resistance of the bridge, rather than any Platonic perfections in it, that finally win the admiration of the poet. Through the years during which he knows the bridge, it sustains, rather than repels, difference, composing itself anew as tourists pass over it: "An Indian bevy, ivory reliefs, / glide careless of the scene as though their lives / were full of willows and small wavy bridges."

However, thirty years later, the bridge turns out to need rebuilding, and the poet is anxious: "Will you in all complacence reappear / well set up tubbed and innocent of soul / as simulated Gothic?" He is reassured, finally, by thinking of the bridge "as toy", an image that might be represented "in three fine squiggles of a Chinese brush", a sign, like the miniature Tang warrior unearthed from a tomb, of something "in smallness larger than / all gods and life."

"The Bridge" is a poem of local piety, then, but also a poem hailing the imperfect work of the builder's art as solace and symbol, much as 'The Willow" joins the piety of an address to a household god to a celebration of the sheer organic power of natural growth. Those who make the acquaintance of Arthur Sale through these two poems will enter willingly into the other poems here, finding a poet who combines cerebral investigation with tender vulnerability. They will learn to move within his knotty and even reclusive style, finding that it encloses a visual and emotional responsiveness that threatens to burst its austere bounds of meter. It is that combination of the strict and the intense in Arthur Sale that will draw readers to these profound and changeable poems.

Helen Vendler

The Bridge

The Bridge in Motion

The bridge is always moving moving un-
der arches over levels bevels in
the sunlight from and over itself sliding.
Sometimes the flow pleats to a crest, slants, slats
down like an unwilling Venetian blind,
but mostly as in a print by Hokusai
lazy easy corrugation of flame.

A microscopic core now of disturbance
where final shadow intersects the water
blows billions of bright arcs off, like a whirring
watch spring, with intact centre but with sides
elongating in rising aggrandisement
out of penumbra up the open courses
(shining put in shade and shorn by sunlight) with
concentricity and contact with
the shaping impulse lost, like flimsy fairings
of concertina lattice, shilly shally,
dancing amorphously advance retreat,
a tribal tomtom dart recoil repeat.

Punts chocking by, the bridge plots radiant cables
to check them, vainly, dwindling in the washes
lithe and sly enough for slithery fishes.
Or as the mesh tightens towards adherence
thin spinning parallels like silver birches
come floating free, then sliver, cakewalk, crinkle,
into the quickest craziest graphlines ever
charted the minute fevers of the river.

At any instant in each arch the dance is
different in time, in movement, in direction,
but on all sunwards vertical surfaces
tempos designs and sizes all collapse
into the shapeless routine leap and lapse,
the disa- reappearing repeated

3

unchanging childish joggle on the wall,
the insubstantial rock bottom of things,
monstrous reflections flickering on stone
of atoms in the stone, monotonous
continuous performance of their newsless
spectral collisions: – impossible campaigns
where all are enemies and none allies
and random bombardment never slackens
and the fight is not for freedom but for bonds.
And yet, bewildering reversal of our
world wars, from these intestine jars emerges
not chaos but communicating stone,
a compact bridge is heeled from their loose scrimmage
(Some catspaw comfort accelerates the ripples)
– in what primordial grove does this arch vista
rocking like a bridge of rattan arrive,
where a frail culture of translucent mistletoe
crystals a myth of healing, not of murder?

For now from a world washed flat by total war,
and assenting to the judgement of its flood,
and quite innocent of hope for myself
or salvage, glimpsing in, though not on quest,
this play in air on stone of fire and water
(as if the bridge now made, not spanned, an abyss),
the vision of some pre-organic grail,
abstract, schematic, in-principial,
beyond colour, beyond mass, too calorescent
to transfuse in the crass warmth of the blood:
– half suffering, half blessing the unguessable
emblem, the baffling beating of the dance,
yes, I nod, yes, yes, though bungling the rhythm,
to the ripple under over through the bridge.

Bridge Accosted

O moving bridge perpetual motion bridge,
stand still a moment till I get you down;
your frown
(a sudden cloud) that favour would begrudge,
yet I am no treacher, foreign or from town,

by forced exposure or, still worse, the snap,
through greedy lens to suck your medicine;
no sin
in my design to map in a single rap
your lines (like magnets' lightning sketches in

neat iron dust), then brush your cheek and go,
and you welcome the next guest in the file,
your smile
the same, – but his acknowledgement? I know
he could not celebrate you in such style,

still less assign the same high role to you.
So humour me, my bridge, or I will use
abuse,
call you cakewalk bridge, one of Micky's crew
or ' Bridge by Fougasse ' (and what could be worse ?)
– three waggish triangles of paws, legs, hips.
Quelle blague   And yet the shameful amends due
to you
as it is deemed unlucky to change ships
midsea I'll defer. – Yet I'll risk it too,

except I'll save your curved incumbent curbs,
your semicircles, – in all not one line there
set square,
all aspirations to the perfect orbs
poised on your bevelled ledge – till (if I dare)

once more I pay you calls a shade more grave
and adore in a more adequate tone
your stone
and dark approach, that ancient lime tree grove.
Approach ? Nay, that's the route time past has gone.

And I stand on the middle arch, time present,
sidelong to past and future, but a stride
to each side
so sprightly, light, I cannot feel imprisoned,
and see you not as turnkey but as guide:-

compere to the past but not dry as dust,
eloquent now and despite boasting steel
still
a working model and a gracious thrust
to the future – if we can cease to kill:

if not, compassionately be destroyed
like pets by such a crashing giant trunk
sunk
as late bowled down your angle balustrade,
not by the present's yardstick's, bombstick's, stradd-
le, strung out like your fourfluked pilasters in a rank.

Bridge Arrested

I know the covering spring is late but surely
the plane wilts more in its symmetric bell glass;
limes stagger the skyroads more open-headed,
the mistletoe mop on their untidy map
a dragging cancer, not the procreative
crudely jacked cradle I half hoped; the beech's
springy arthritis of aspiration is
intercepted, turned back, Mandarined
in ungular imploration, and the willows
wail through their Blakean veiling maiden hair.

Even the well-pinned festoons of the bridge
surely they dip more, towards the core and tips ?

What has happened, to the bridge, to my hope ?
What absence from the anniversary
that seems so samefaced ? – Sun ? The sun obliges,
for the mallard drake's viridian glows with the
terrible black flames of stained glass window dragons,
until an arch quenches the burning worm,
and the river, by pretending what is missing
in its own steal, is striving to distract me
from what I miss now – the lapsed pulse of the stone.
Where is the heatless flow through the warmed stone,
the ghostly lancers through my solid blood,
riding rejection to the rhythms of acceptance ?

The dancing bridge, projecting on its screen
atom enlargements, must have taken umbrage,
given up the game. No whirring now, save where
the erect drake's thrust bent back foot
strikes upwards like an opening umbrella
loosening rings of force from the coiled water,
or where the piers set up a calm recoil
of water held at arm's length by itself
in softest fosses; but the bridge keeps adamant.

Was it my levity you answered, bridge,
(when I required your stillness for a moment)
by this tragic unshakable compliance ?

If so, inspecting now without distraction
of the pop-gun bombardments of your pulse
your ranked pilaster pawns (that, promoted,
pack into castles as perspectives close)
without a cheer and without cause for cheer
(unless in sudden confoundment they should
re-pulse into action, return to the charge)
I praise the steady beauty of these troops,
but with irony appropriate to an
official enquiry into lost elan,
till frigid scrutiny, confronted by
(O face-warming, O face-saving discovery!)
the pontic arms, volatilises in
the fire brightly burning on that shield
(held where the ranks superbly hoist head high
cannon-ball fossils in perpetual peace)
flames that an antique Stuart chisel felt
leak from the stone like blood under its bite,
and, happily to staunch them, petrified them;
and against which now a butterfly is aptly
sucked like a sheet of opened newspaper
drawn in the fire it was meant to draw.

Such unexpected and miraculous find
of hoary confirmation momentarily
subverts the commonsense of the commission,
impersonates the absence it confirms,
whisks out of ash a sudden flaring prayer
for the greater miracle of restoration.
Can a kiss awake the heart and can that set
wagging the clockwork palace once again ?
Can we resume at the point where we left off ?

Idolatry crawls back under the ashes,
for restoration is the saddest idolon
of all the circular dictionary hopes.
The angle balustrade the giant trunk
huffed down, has it not suffered it ? Enough
that restoration is now its antonym,
which is at least a verbal miracle.

Nor can other miracles revive what died
when the atom music's compass was reversed,
and the approved indefinitely ductile
ligaments of the body of the dance,
beyond earthlong endurance elongated
by a fanatical new dancing master,
snapped with no twang (for tone cracked in the act)
but with a sick slap and a stockinged thud
that rent the nerves and eardrums of the world,
harrowed the prophets of the belly pit's
primordial presentience of the end,
caused, not this bridge from chaos, but caused chaos.

Between this year and that, your faith and mine,
all couplings, ties, all arches that are more
than means to ferry you from here to there,
ends, not dead ends, though rooting eyes and feet
to their own meditated packed articulate rights,
an organic dictation by the water,
the littorals, and the need to correlate them,
between all catalysts and beneficiaries
and elemental symbioses of
water and earth and air and flame and man,
and through the shrinking adamant of fate,

falls the invisible atom falling
on Nagasaki, on Hiroshima.

Second Anniversary

Highest in memory for sun and snow
flood followed by drought, although the year mandates
its biggest guns of light to celebrate
my annual bridge party, that honour's put
neglected by, now that the secret is out.

Although the light, alert with hazelessness,
disinterestedly detecting your face
for age, unmarked like dog pads in wet concrete
until irreversible petrification,
toothcombs you all in vain and in fact sleeks you,
I am not gratified, for timelessness,
now that the secret's out, is pointlessness.

On your survival of that lethal winter
— against and under snow, snow picking out
your sagging lineaments, haggard you looked,
a soiled creased elephant in the dazzling circus,
solemn under incongruous white frills —
congratulations mob your door but only
Pandora-like to let your secret out.

Later in thaw mobilised into floods
drawn to a higher head by wind, I saw
you sunk and fighting white-gilled for your life,
in the ripping swaying shocking express current
scratching its timber claws along your palate
and gnawing knees to make you lift your feet,
with flying buttress wings shored only on
evasive lakes, and yet you held you held
those butting shoulders down under your springy arch,
and trial to gain, tragic to comic, turned,
for the hump-backed monster slobbering your keystones
springcleaned recesses, restored the pinks and creams
that bloom so vacuous now the secret's out.

For today as the first noticed time upstream
but transriparian I neared there broke
on me the difference that in many a print
of you I'd denied as the graver's fault
not yours, now curse my blindness not the graver's.

— In summer reclination as in a punt
so graciously disposed — instead of that
continent undulation I stumbled on
a hedgehog creature serialled and cored
with sharp disjunctions unsurmountable
except by passengers along their hunched
and slumped lie across the stream. I wrong
you, bridge, but shock and recence claim that right,
of undeclared and unsuspected darts
the rankle in the celebrating flesh.

You do not flow . . . From my old trusted view
in lovely unindulgent curves the force
swings back into the past: from here exposed
your hackles overjut the reverse climber
returning to be broken on the ridges.
You jolt the past back like a cakewalk from
the future: you do not connect: angles
abrupts from here: from there all circulation:
— two diverse-storied profiles like a face,
that is your secret, patent now it's out.

But come, despite two faces you are not
Jekyll and Hyde: this second birthday card,
banal like all, need not be baneful too.
though the last arch's outmost pier is not
flexibly free, as I had dreamed, to sense
and fasten on the future with an elephant's
taper prehension, or the caterpillar's
erect circumflexion at the leaf tip
before the next descending visitation
and looped adhesion across the abyss:
and though your reconcoction, with connivance

11

of sun and river, of the sunward pattern
once dandled something in my lymph (not blood),
is ghastly coquetry, and anyway
ungainly dancing days are done (I was
an antipodean casualty, you know,
of Nagasaki and Hiroshima);
and though the future may not dance your step;
and you, like mortals, have impulsions and
elbowy repulsions, a fair face and the one
turned from admirers : yet still you are best
of bridges, I worst fool to wrestle from you
in an increasingly schematic world
anything but your solid settled beauty,
and in this timed and ticking impermanence
to cerebrate and abstract your compact mass
and autarkic minute particulars
by allegory and symbol, in far fetched
distortions foist my own moods on, or praise, you
except for what you are and that you are
in the untouchability of things
daily distending in grey rarefaction
from day to unexpected day,   still there.

Third Anniversary

The flow is on; a sparrow from the ball
cheeps, and the mated ducks sleep end to bill,
dirigibles of rest above the stream
whose rock and drift the beam
(a patterned and a curled Tahitian prow)
balancing on a pier will not betray.
Nor will the sun what plane and willow will,
whose reflections like oil
(but use contrasted) pick out, plan, construct,
as in a picture by Cezanne, the rocked
drift in loose rafts and erect envelopes.
And look, look, the prelaps-
arian pulsings in the bridge's reins!

The flow is on; only with tenderest greens
knotting its lashes only the sallow bodes
birds', hearts', and buds'
desert or fall. Duly then from whose image
skimming the surface but seeming to emerge
from gulfs resurgent, I observe the bridge
has only couples rich
each in each, not in trophies of the scene.
No solitary with the silent sign
leans on the parapet to constrict desire
from wide arch to a wire
of icy vertebration and a thin dress –
to my half-grieved relief, for I confess
venery of Ver would, weak as I am,
distract me from my aim.

Then (undistraction happy and apposite)
seeming to drain all couples from the sight
flowing across the bridge cap-a-pe dressed
in silks burning abreast,
an Indian bevy, ivory reliefs,
glide careless of the scene as though their lives

were full of willows and small wavy bridges
with broadly bevelled ledges
soft edged like Scotch pancakes and underlapping
in inverse terraces down-inwards sloping.

These minute red green sunflower-coloured queens
so alien at once
strangely belong; half indifferently half
waveringly ranging the bridge they have
its own behaviour; their exotic glow
suits its; no megalo-
maniac jut (though an innocuous bore)
of dragon's teeth from that lank chapel's jaw,
but enough life in small design to fill
a dozen such naves full.

Better than neighbouring King's these remote queens
affirm familiarly as the swans
playing their curves' insatiety of store
off on the moving floor
my bridge's shapes, proportions, integrations,
climbs and declines, sculptures and right relations.
That silken heraldry above the bridge
sharpens or quickens knowledge
(like spectacles when vision blurs and greys
or varied limelights picking up degrees
levelled else in interim fugs and fogs)
of pontic paradox: –
convention transcending into rarity,
into unity contrariety,
naif urbanity, practised spontan-
eity, transpontine
transporting tenderness with tremendous might.
– Might ? Stand either short of the bridge and sight
both scalloped parapets, which scale and fall
like the great China wall,
or wide and low: – lower one seems to start
but higher climbs, and where they cross a state
of power seems declared, imperial strength
generated in lack-length.

That Eastern silks, pilaster pawns between,
ahead, askance, – rights of a chessboard queen, –
gliding its span, can make even more clear
the candour of my Clare
must have a moral (Cultures when they clash
are mutual touchstones too, exposing trash,
enhancing and, the better by contrast scaled,
characterising gold ?),
but on this sensuous morning the mere tale
seems sense enough, seems true, however tall,
and grateful in this foreign greetings card
I hail the luck which could
grant me both freedom from that breeding ruck
and in this small bright antique map to track
unnoticed feats and features of my bridge
lost to an unapt age.

Yet out of such contrast such congruence
who could have dreamt ? Or (like paradox) that Wren's
bridge's derivative congruence should yield
only plain contrast, modelled
fair as it is on Clare, all whose festoons
are ironed rigid and whose springing stance
has fallen like flat feet, and hard
its elegance, and dead
as pontifex, constructed strips sold per
the arch like perforated stamps, a peer
not even in power, for Clare's pilasters seen
sans weakening space between
are staved, in cross-set serried concave edges,
in by the strataed coping's pressure ridges –
a frieze of crowded copious and resilient
potence which impotent
the right line's rule, the tyranny
of tension are to copy or deny.

These balanced lessons, of my pontic study
have made the vision steady,
less tampered with behind the retina

by fears and hopes that infect scrutiny –
and may the bridge, as with its own blood mortared
an Indian infant murdered
to placate river gods, in the deep quicks
of infant bridges, might corrupt all the bricks –
a cupboard skeleton whose covert grin
softened not safened grain.

But through contrasted lenses is restored
the true object, no longer throbbed and stirred
to my internal tunes, the spreading stain
erased from every stone.

Like in unlike   and contrast in resemblance
providing both the black ground and the brilliance,
floodlight my bridge, with no distraction from
its florid sexual frame
and eyes' innocent bridges across chasms
between mind's images and macrocosm's,
enabling those to impersonate these.

But now I see with eyes,
not fears and hopes, the rampant pontic limbs
white as unicorns and sweet; the lace hems
whose intervals being better than the real
balustrade, so reveal
its excellence: reflections that subtend
(solid as) arches and complete their round:
plants lodged on ledge and plinth: – all pristine, all new
as the bronze beech leaves which now
(copper against sun, green where they keep the shade)
at taper candelabra tips tearing the shard
jet like gas flares, but with a tenderness
that leaves their down no less.

The Bridge Rebuilding
or
Thirty Years After

The worst bridge in the world not made of rattan
slacker of joint and harder to replace.
"Loose stones in string bags?" String courses in iron
and iron like Alice a mushroom and a room
puffs as it rusts up out of place releasing
bond after bond, like knives around pie crusts
or an addicted thumb down card deck edge
or dandelions weight-lifting compact tarmac,
tieing the bridge tieing me to the bridge
three years may be, from muddy soles of piers
to coping sealed with lichen, block by block
extracted serviced and restored. "Say three
say too the untieing took three hundred years."
So threats renewal without cleats to dowel
more surely than mortar or mortice askew.
"That undulation, silk skeined loping hound
slowed down then frozen in a line of beauty
that clears the slick from its commercial bilge
or, brush in charge as cox and nearly eight,
a grounded squirrel hurrying to take off
or an event in dolphinry Olympics
all fluent as their bearing brine or blade,
at least was part and parcel of the plan
these crimp irons clinch. Relax is not relapse
as deem deriders who see keystones slipping
through parting cement finger tips into
the under hug and tug these hundred years.
What architect should fathom engineer
was conscript to prevent?" Good tradesmen all
off to the wars left sluggards layabouts
to play at bricks. For planes and chisels slugs
as in flamingo croquet I'd engage
to line shine sharpen and to gouge reliefs:

look at Arion, Irish harp and all
at sea on a whale, think of cathedral swine
rising like fish to corniced acorns. Where you
unaltered beauty find I there the fault
where downed tools were snatched up to overtake
a week's blind and halt.

                            "Expertly thus destroyed
before one ball is off the balustrade
where is my bridge and were you ever mine?
Refurbished inchmeal as demolished where
with whom will appeals lodge? Will soul cling on
though but the soul of my imagined bridge
in freed interstices by scrapped iron bars
built in at once as stays built in as death,
and bind instead, like babes interred alive
to ancient bridges strong boxed sentinels
against surprise by rising river gods?
Will you in all complacence reappear
well set up tubbed and innocent of soul
as simulated Gothic? That profile turned
from devotees I once discerned is what
a master mason last of the old breed
would like Picasso depict in surcharge
full face and side in one – a foolish one?"
At least unlike those tomfool Stuart bodgers
you bear too hard with too sharp edge. As bridge
the visage is 'tis true only a mask
the complex posture of a marionet
in harmony and shapeliness pegged out
by strings invisible at every joint
sine qua non.   But joy itself it is
as toy, an elephant all rag and stuff
a child might clamber on, or a fancy bridge
in three fine squiggles of a Chinese brush;
or a T'ang rider tiny as absolute
cut out by laser from the unearthly end
of his millennial corridor, frail
as infrangible, in smallness larger than

all gods and life. – "The opportune arrival
Westerns affect, not least this Eastern-Western,
to save the day.   So you and I through art
may have our bridge and eat our words opposed
– if that can rehabilitate." That rests
with me three years.

Miscellaneous Poems

A Horizontal Afternoon

I wake but cannot rise.
Though the Sun, a busy all about me mellow nurse,
unfurls me warmly lubricating knees,
featherily bolsters me upright
with long strong rods and rays,
injects but sympathises, wrestles but agrees –
despite caress and prod
I cannot rise.

Though Conscience is called in –
professional bonhomie and parsonic bray –
"Congratulations first on looking spry;
from such recuperative nap
no danger of a cold on
rising up, gently now . . ." – despite all that's skilled in
levitation and snoop
I stay skull down.

Approached by Interest
with pencil tapping on my bedrail, can I pay
in full but if unfortunately poor
up, and the sooner the better,
for general strikes uncrossed
contract the general ataxia of the crazed –
– the flatter for bread and butter
crises I rest.

Though in Grand Chorus, "Rise!"
sings life and fair occasion, "Rise!" sing religions
morphologies moralities delusions
diligence hygiene and the main chance –
these chants framed to rouse, drowse
me, till unknown unnamed a voice that same word "Rise!"
carelessly as it mentions
surprised I rise.

'Neither fear nor courage saves us'

Is it enough to say that
I am a coward and the
harsh voice from the road the
gate rocking the rubber footsteps on the concrete
the dead knock on the shaking door are but
the casual visitor the baker's boy and I need
have no fear of   ?

no fear

Is it enough to say my nerves are
bad and at night the
whispering on the road the
swishing grass outside the veiled French windows
the clear tapping on the undulating window are but
the wind the rat the scratching twig and I need
have no fear of   ?

no fear

Is it enough to declare that
I am neurotic craven and that
all I fear is the policeman the
glasshouse the snooper the collector for
spitfires the red cross the salvage the battleships and these
        mean
the loss of cash only or freedom or life and I need
have no fear of   ?

no fear

It is not enough to declare these
facts or these fancies
for I have heard
inside the fears and the uniformed voices a minute question
rocking our foundations splintering our entrances the
       held out
telegram by the wind or the messenger boy requiring
                         an answer or

no answer

Noah Stylites

Those brisk and roric walks, unnecessary
aperitifs before the porridge, grapefruit,
bacon and eggs, before the Second Flood
was more than a mud geysir in the East,
a resort of unwholesome fascination.

The gear laid out and kettle on the fire,
I filled my free half hour up with freedom
on empty road and path, while the lithe bitch,
disdaining scents the dew had snuffed out first,
untrodden yet by new, broke the trail for me,
her long poised tail swaying like a censer
between the live pillars of that intact Eden,
to where the old man, stub arms along the
iron bridge rail, leaned across sewage smells,
the only favours of the naked ditch,
to the green other slope, in hopes of seeing
some old drake tread an accommodating fowl –
"I seen 'em oft, me and this little maid"
(several rails down but staring just as hard).

Sometimes we'd meet him splayfoot on the path,
cursing each single stone with stick and tongue:
"The sod, as laid these pebbles without sand!
They'll ne'er bed down till winter wet, they'll be
the death o' me." He died, I saw him last
on his last walk, just crawling from a hedge
and from a fit, an independent, earthy,
oathy little man, drab face, drab clothes,
but money in the bed, a retired farmhand,
who told the farmers on his beat his mind –
Tractors too heavy for that galt, two horses
one horse too many, steam ploughs were the best.
He ran his crone round almost at his last gasp,
whose screeches fetched his sons from doors away
to haul him off.

It was then I dropped my walks,
leaned on the garden gate, the dog daring me
till habit tamed her, hailed the timid roadman,
who prowled on his safe stretch of road and talked
wisely of war, eyes busy pendulums
towards the unlikely passing of his boss.

But now the fens were flooded, I took to
latching the gate, retreated in good order
back up the garden slope, turned the big key,
and looked out from the window at the waste,
my eyes bleared by illusions of land in
the sewage crust and faces in the flotsam,
feeling the waters' impure ablution
warren like rodents in my cracked foundations
ventilating storey after storey
(as they will comb a rotted down forgotten
bean-stack into a vibrating skyscraper).

Then left the look-out unmanned, settled myself
full length on this broad comfortable settee,
and watched only cracks, how they multiply
in that Nile flood of fertilizing blood,
waxing on walls now crazy paved like a tapped
eggshell, of that neat radiating creeper
with its minute ingrown dichotomy
themselves the mere interstices shored up
by the mercurial mass of their destroyer,

walls mortared once as fondly as once Melville
stitched his thick patchwork White Jacket
(a handy house complete with airing cupboards)
for lack of the essential caulking pitch
into a mortal liability
when inside safety's buoyant fling he struggled
in its and the waves' immobilization.

The Mist

As the infinite series of recurrent dream
sidles to its interminable terminus
the endless train draws up along the endless platform
but never close enough to stop,
it must, surely it must, fouling at the Nth term the point
    the limiting sum
and quietly leaving the rail~look I have
returned escaped, I am awake and never changed.

And while outside the mist lasts nothing is changed, no lost
ticket's recurrent number is missed, for the mist
blocking yet opening out the twi-casemented window
into a decreasingly truncated cone
sucks like a conjuror's hat into its adaptable envelope of
    vacuum
the protracted ordinates of dream, and even
even before involuntary eyes can bear the dragging
abyss, the dreaded opening lesson of the day,
and the chronic pain turn over, painlessly
the painful pressure root of the recurrent crack
opening above and below the window
(as if the wall should be cracked and not the picture on it)
is drawn out by undroning suction, or at least the nerve is
    numbed.

And in this tranquil
O so freshly mopped clean discharge of guilt a house
inveterately divided against itself, settled
down into comfortable halves, into a separation
mutual and unrancorous, is a solution
as acceptable and unremarkable as a halved cake, while
the mist holds soft possession and the strong impression no
crack can grind its edges on my heart.

Relief is now the signature rippling across the wall
and even the void glass interval cannot void it,
for along the inset graphlines with quick change of plane
    and plan
and a carte-blanche ticket to infinity flashing
from indefinity it rejoins at the top of the window
the crack line regiment it never left, but where
trick-riding its asymptote it returns —
changing surely state not train —
is unplottable as the point of awakening, impossible
as to bring the crack's wry planes to one table: no
matter now for now
the crack sides keep the general peace
(while mist persists and vacuum holds) not cheek by jowl
but by the defile and abyss between them,
definitive issue and resolve of forces, and
scrawl on the wall, though touching on infinity, is
(unlike Balshazzar's) harmless because legible,
as the sickeningly seamless uncrackable crib of neurosis
yawns with relief at the simple recalled combination,
until
only just until the reticulate mist haul off, call
its pipistrell decoy in,
the gin.

A Transformation Scene

Bidden to the christening of a heart I entered
a silver spoon
hot in my hand but my spine
prickled as though the infant to be fonted
instead were to be interred.

And indeed the service (unexpected as had been
the birth itself) seemed haunted
if not quite as I hinted,
for firstborn so late less a boon
might prove than bane.

But despite fears he might turn stubborn
he made not the least fuss
until his face
under the water that is dipped each babe in
seemed on a sudden to burn.

For the liquid steamed and even the parson fainted
when in a warning voice
that rang inside the holy vase
Euhoe! he cried, Euhoe! as he vented
(though that may have been unintended)

over the holy man, who not at all offended
restored thus from his faint
round the slopping font
in wreath of stone and belly still more distended,
with transformed bystanders banded,

danced to an organ pipe. Meanwhile the well oiled babe
cool and counter to the hubbub
swam till my head span,
then changed the water, in the tub,
with one part mother's milk to sillabub
for all to bib.
Whereat I yielded and ladled away with my spoon.

"I *must devise*"

I must devise an image of my pain
once shape size source are known. The source is fear
(thousands of fears), the shape and size are me,
the whole not like a bespoke parasite
ubiquitously battening on me, but
I inspiring on approval through my lungs,
familiar countenanced at my own meat,
and each dictated act enlarging like
a film trailer's expressionless hyperbole
from not some goat stance in the ravined brain
but its own special correspondent fear
which makes for confidence.
                            The country's trade
under the occupation is in pain,
which, rivalries and opposites absorbed,
now acts as their sole representative
in kindest compensation.
                            And of this fool-
proof most incorruptible monopoly
I am the trademark which I must devise.
· That known it needs only to be reborn.

"The Universal"
or
Popular Science

The Universal was as much the first
vacuum machine as it will be the last
will be in fact the universe at least.

By some patent device or knack, difference
that blows prestige into supremacy,
it needs nor wheels nor shaft but stops at home,
all stomach inside and all stomach out,
and all in sight or flight drops in. Mass falls
gas falls, light years and passing light pitch
into the pit and fail to reappear,
tick atom particle ray wave or charge
from this dark dock of space never to emerge.

Most of the universe, mages aver,
Is in this hole or worse, of galaxies
the furthest off now lacks such size our eyes
could track it were it young we old enough,
the rest could use a hundred eyes instead
of two for instant view, our milky way
would floodlight night and day, but (mentors fear)
must render as it is ten score a year
of the best suns, our suns, to the clueless maw
of some good neighbourhood minotaur.

                                                    Yet

the remainder hardware in that bankrupt sky,
though good for only twopence in the pound,
still meets foreseen demands, and mages give
answers truer than accounts, as witness, poor
Pluto at every census loses mass,
descends from God to Oberon the yob,
a moon that Neptune lost and not his peer

and will decline by decimation, if
scales refine still, into its own avernus,
annihilated by bad sums and not
the wary wavy wars of collapsed stars
stripping the gravitation each from each
as in a pane a wasp through pointed arches
of a crane fly thigh crunches after thigh.

Mass breakage too is no more astronomical
Universal than in life's small family firm:
an annual investment in creation
each individual daily act with means
to overpopulate the earth, a birth
at most, most often nought, for sole return,
sees crawl from that black cul de sac, for all
the thousand worlds like a wet booted ball
spuming with spunk shot in, or that one life
itself good but for nothing: null or nil.

If so small nature inconceivable
energies of unconception can accept
the Black Death pitting the whole universe
may die itself before its stellar hosts
of swollen belly with the winds of nothing;
or the bubbles of this colic, this Nirvana,
articulated by their radiation, be
templates and temples of new masses so
mass may be nothing finding its own form
in measurements too negative for rule,
and time takes such a tumble as to serve
not even as a humble bracket curve
in the equation of negation with creation,
or the convenient lettering of a line
in the pure geometry of empty space.

But while the dear old Universal drives
the big game milling in its bag, pelt flesh
horn roar callow or hoar, svelte warded bone,
yet shakes no emptied Humpty Dumpty out

or vanished grin but (for these magic days
theories proliferate as the poem writes)
the latest cry in the last materials – bales
in a trice like an ice in the larruping
tongue of an allover Disney dog cas-
cading into a smoke of veils, so keeps
far hence still chained the Fenris Wolf – less chance
ill chance attends the macrocosm out –
riding on honed edges ages full
of red leech cups only to be about
to be sepulchred in this droning hoover
the microcosm's last fling and break through,
most pileate housepride that must tidy at
all costs saving its own, clean nouveau riche
sweeps all before it in the common ditch
so cocksure of its everlasting niche
earthquakes are not unwelcome now and then
provided thickest in thickest walks of men
to make new rooms or brooms; or as Keats said
"What a pity, Haydon," (exclamation-marked
with the alpha plus of genius by whom)
"What a pity there is not a human dust hole."

Safe Transference

Out of encompassing windows waking
into the summer dawn from grounded sleep
eyes shiver naked on the edge of all
those aromatic spouts and ringing cascades
in dread of battery and inadequacy.

But like a world on a gold pendant hanging
crystalline rondures of the light bulb hold
safe safe the polar window nodes, the whole
exploding summer, and the humming fly
switching his orbits like a boy in the
commensurate fairground of his dreams awaking.

The Tree

" The tree I remember best, the hollow
an eyesore, unofficial public dump
to fill the pond, once skatable, called 'Reedy'.
But the elm tree hardly saw, roots drove clean under,
such rammle. It stood back high – "   It stood across
my French windows, so close they opened on it.
" Fell, I suppose, missing the house, luckily
a low one? Elms are treacherous on this galt
bedrocked on subterranean lakes. "   No, cut.
" It came to that? Took no doubt more than due
of what sunshine was going ? "   Almost too high
and too high-branched to shade it.   " Spoilt the view
from the wide windows? "   No view except in winter
(we made the hedge grow tall), in winter only
of rotten sheds, roofs for the rats' holes, and,
sole relic of its shed, a turnip cutter.
" If less view was no loss, why must the tree fall? "
Because the bungalow's foundation was
lodged on the broad back of one of the roots.
" Sounds safe – an extra beam to bear the house,
or keel to ride the laminal underland sea. "
A knife to slice the house through like a cake.
That tree, bent to the gale like a full sail
spread miles, dangerous vibrating miles, above
the squat safe house, by infinitesimal
displacement, a tremor through the roots could, would,
snap the house clean as a clay pipe stem.   " True
as seismograph a house might be what most
could be desired – except the cost. So roost
must fall in case the rooster should. I see
more in the danger than in the solution.
A rip-saw spitting through that root had saved
a day's grunt at the trunk, the house, the tree. "
Too late to think of that. Besides, the tree
was too grand for the house, made it look mean.
Besides, I like, yes I do like, to see

the turnip cutter chop the winter sun
brought close by frost and brightened like a mangold.
" One can buy safety at too low a price. "
Not if it is safety, but safety has
a shell-proof shelter lies lower than truth
and as unvenial.   " You mean – ? "   I mean
look at my house with low safe precautions
leaded and shelled and underpinned and cracked
neat as an egg on a basin rim, spilt gold,
and irrecoverable as Humpty Dumpty.

High Jinx

Three years it grew   in sun and shower   at ten
a hand could rock it   and it still not weep
     my willow   when its standard went off gold
then   ridge poles reached around and laths declined
venetian shutters   vertical   half cock
paling the light   Moulded   the dome filled   out
and up   bellying   like a swayed balloon
     so furious   the fire   in that gut
hydraulic fire   that is   a residence
desirable   but always   to be sold
in lane   and clover leaf   and city   fissioned
imperial boulevards and arteries
metropolis   and megalopolis
unoccupied   beneath the empty bowl

And where the burghers   musically hedging
house and estate   and what wings fold   and stay?
Even tourists land   in single ignorance
no guided flocks   and birds of passage only
is all   too airless   or too air conditioned
like a bell jar   or that Buckminster Fuller's
city's encased and insulated climate
or inbuilt treachery   in every cell
like Asgard   so   strong roads snap off   as in
Steinberg   or Piranesi gaols   or nests
swing into space   like fairground whirligigs
or exudation   salicine   and fatal
as from dry powder architectonics
of After London   or of gridded carriage
the complete lack
                    Now   at the golden wedding
breaking the spell   whatever   of no marriage
storming the undefended citadel
for show   and joy   along uncumbered roads
two storm cocks   larger than life thrushes   take
bravado   and brave   royal possession

Here fix our flag   first of our reign   and from
proper concern   Our Line   should show concern
we build homogenous   with osier slips
in rising circlement   like spinning clay
and palace roof   skull cap in due accord
no problem   it is us
                    And when the storm
our element   Our House's Arms   beats down
true workmen   we take time off   for as true
Royals   we have millennial time to spare
for   this   is Eden   peepshow to the mob
or rogue reporter   but that we should lack
no precedent   lo here   the undulating squirrel
standing on tiptail come to case the joint

(At *the suggestion of* Eamonn *Duffy*)

Tit Chat

This longtailed tit   there are no residents
or travellers   now   you must have sent   to gaze
not stare   although the neatest of lorgnettes
with such   rare benignance   at me from the twig
all boughs   are twigs on this unaging birch
that never silverplates into adulthood
and there is nothing in it for the tiniest
tot of a bird   to preserve peach complexion
and the coconut that   many branched as is
the tit connexion   could embrace them all
under its dome of glittering restaurant
still barrels the ambrosia in rough wood
that might have homed him here   as moths perfume.
You   then   out of your mammoth neighbourhood
knowing our dearth   or why steadfast these clawlets
as light   as fresh   as tears to lids   allaying
smouldering anxiety   that sabotage
perpetual motion of head   beak   and tail?
More than guessed kindness and demure affection
this mini despatch means   when his aged perch
a minor was   my March dusks checked their watches
each lingering minutes longer along elder
polled elm and winterbourn   that passed for hedge
with our raw house   by a kit of his forebears
like engineers up in the telegraphs
a brisk work force at their last port of call
as tergiverse   from pressures to clock out
to safety measures against dangerous me
as to my meek "goodnight"   a point   a name
at least we were on their maps   if only as
a raiding target for their crowded clans
that fearless age of sun and slump   the tramp
was half the world past our white gate   and half
the night was nightingales   when sirens blared
to share their watches   how would I curse those rounds
drowning the sirens   of most musical sounds

like refined water torture in old China
lambasting drums   from where that bird is now
with clamour that made taut brains ring like wine
glasses   and break   who would half welcome   now
even the sirens if they brought that song.

Accidental Voices

I have been driven inwards more and more
like a clumped pile by gravity's steel heel
stamped on for years. O saving passive voice
that makes necessity paralysis
from dancing choice, as now, December dawn,
cock clock and blackbird striking together
not wake make record but slip me in resleep
down to deny ouverture to the world
so sharing with creation only doom.

Heard acted out over the netted globe
what arousal what erection what exertion
remedial exercises might dictate
the radio active voice.

        Quack sublimate
this screwed leaf scribbled with compassionate leave
corona peering round complete eclipse,
ratchet fanged rim to eyeball bare too limp
to graph or limn the bubbling gold elixir
in fractional black out containment by
that taut retort   just held.

Art & Algy:
In All The Realms Of
Non Sense Absolute

Metronome betwixt polarities
of maps and palimpsests the lengths of corridors
gaze held out stiffly as a blind man's wand
books the last thing on his mind but through space
concentration powering to enforce
one binary recalcitrant black star
to spin That or the universe was wrong

What coil rewinding from what whip could lash
gyre that peg top Why mind and fitness sensed
as incontrovertible by such men
as Darwin braved his bared head marvelling
at the storm's tug of war with those absorbing
bryony bed springs to uncoil as from
a whaling tub the rope runs free   as vainly
as his own hypochondriac bed's recall

And this the mix   though fatal here folk joke
for in the far camp of Prince Relativity
his eyes undeviating from the skies
forgot the straying feet   that is   as well
the build   the template the raw stuff   of verse
conceived and helixed   on impossibles
matter of factly   as the painted bricks
of children's toys   ranging the universe
but homely in the hand as a ripe apple
or as happy counter part   the atom
that keeps for ever and a day in play
any thing in the world one can invent
and make of parts that spring from brain to hand
and cell so crinkled and so stoked within
broached like a jinnee from a bottle would
shake out into a sun radiant or black

Such paradox and poesie walk hand
in hand   no awkward questions asked   process
with image   one   though science for amusement
in need of an accountability
mocks its own proof of quod absurdum est
by quia absurdum   where the Muse merely
whipperganninies blithely for the nonce
as   mandrakes moan in every lifted root
in bestiaries underground   and under ground
or widdershins   the riddles that confute
the Daylight Alice   are Yggdrasil's roots
witness The square root pegged in its round hole
of minus one   that undermines sanity
but props the world   Nothing upon nothing
that   cheeky as the tramper's pebble   serves up
the cosmic soup   where parallels immersed
lose their aloofness in a warm hob nob
Whereas   dichotomising endlessly
aggregates   sidling to their berthing   never
fingers of greeting dwindling with the gap
make fast A sphere has sides   infinite sides
Straight lines cannot be right   but a triangle
is a straight line   No wonder light limps being
both dot and line   So its Olympic gold
world record mandatory unbeatable
for speed despite   bend in its tracks it must
like a lost traveller on his endless plain
And space which as in early signs   may prove
a serpent over running its own tail
Also an afterthought *sine qua non*
like bindweed   binaries are every where
below above and but and ben   and as
inextricable as anti matter
that shadow doppelganger without which
disconsolate as Schlemihl   matter is
Atoms play fives   particular theorists say
sixes then sevens   but not to fear results
threatening jobs for this is but the crackling
and always the next slice off the atom joint
awaits its eights and nines

So "Let's pretend"
that creates real equations equates too
with poet's ploy   product   with procedure
of the same mould in both   imagined real
and real imaginary   for poetry
the fundamental *imprimatur* in
the universe of nothing upon nothing

Nettles

Contracting iron can castigate gone walls
upright into grace, yet purchase must depend
all on the prehensility of its ends
that keeps like Struwwelpeter's ungulance
or patterned forces in a magnet's field
proliferating after the iron stops –
long S, or X, Greek crosses, solar crowns
crinate like Mithra's great and fuming pate
in nether Bath. Young nettles as I passed
seemed suns as sharp-tongued as those metal flowers
on whose sea-anemone's raking clutch
transverse rods haul the slack boat-house waist in,
offering in fine convergence on a wall
crutch or a flying buttress, under sleight
of an ascending testudo that seemed
to invest and not defend, each scale snipped out
by sidelong light as by a pastry cutter,
frail as gold leaf but shattering in its tail.

Leaves' concave pricking orderly beauty, stems'
near-horizontal sympathy with the wall,
that halted me when higher roses did not,
in an old seascape's even dance transporting
on thorned imponderable transparent waves,
must have been nonage, urtic innocence,
virginity or even a trick of light,
undesiccated air, for one day later
the leaves held dust and sand instead of light,
rank and aim broken, and next day the stalks
visible now like the strings of a wrecked piano;
angrily straggled away from the wall.

'Fostered Alike . . .'

"Tell them   and they don't mind"   said tenderest
and sweetest she   as I snapped off the flowers
and herbs   for her delight   her dishes   and
her love   and under shock and salve I thought
not   as one after   might   of harvesters
asking a billion corn in cob a blessing
as good as dead   with orderly back doors
delivering bread   or   with as keen incisors
and warm and fragrant sighs   of meadow kine
that wrench and rasp   or the disturbing blenching
tabled in oriental labs   from loss
of limb assault   or the vicinity
of callousness   in humblest plants   but of
the spring when first my boyhood burst aware
of the enjoyed familiarity
with stream   and dumble   kennels   stables   roads
landmarking larch   and coveted wild flowers
as beauty   too.   That March of hushed dusks
was a first world   that fifty marches since
have served but to serve preservation orders
save by recession   to accentuate
nonentities   that   as a brush lays down
layer on lucid layer   or burnished grain
still can define   refine   by increase and
decrease at once   through shining atmospheres
of separation   wonder and origin.
"Yet   with opacity   in all appearance
enough   to paint out that brutality
in wonder   "   By the strong and dreaded side
and by his wish   the first remembered such
that may have helped   I trod the ideal lanes
of rousing other world   and all his hands
held stones   to stun glimpsed drowsy hedgerow birds
whose song possessed him so   to murder   rather
than not possess   caged   in full bloodied song
inside his storied house   having already
a many songsters   caught   in trap or net.

47

Birch Hats

And their hats were o' the birk

It neither grew in syke nor ditch
Nor yet in ony sheugh
But at the gates o' Paradise
That birk grew fair enough

Harpo's capacious slack   White Jacket stocked
bagsful of tricks   pig for a pick   a lampost
convenienced for lapdogs   beating their bounds
netted like sticklebacks   So   neighbour birch
scarce younger   not much taller   than myself
       bristle cone pines   victorious by a bristle
is   too   like me   a silver adolescent
and   angle in girth   cast line spray   leaves fry
likewise   to toy scale   even to the birds

None welcome   whether fit or free   upon it
grosser than   troy   than feather   -weight   the tit
exclusive hostel   to that coterie
tom   willow   cole   longtailed   tadpole in pink
oxeye   black sheep or troll   oscillating
overpoised   overbearing   overborne
on springboard hair   Wrens even barely touch

down   on a flight   rare now   a flash of fire
or splodge of gold   that dodges nought but notice
By preference tangential   other wings
as   by compulsion swift's   to everything

But   what the affinity   of bird to tree
still more   of tree to bird   is as unsure
as elms   those unsure trees   to rookeries
Sparrows   alone   gate crashing   with intent
exasperate   to mimicry   of guests
on a tit bit treasure search invited   in

coverts of birch   random but fleet as e'er
a hirondel's through mited air   So will
this band of copycats   on winter thistles
stand   off and on   while the provoking bullfinch
a bulb of crimson   in a Noel pane
scorches to cores   and then   through chiding chatter
and mime   as nullified   as winnowed down
his full fat whistle flutes

                        So though there be
pigeons for pines   helmets of elm for rooks
      any dichotomy is dorm   to stares
indefinite enough   and calm for crow
bare bole   spare arms   like almonds blanched   hoar roof
to cap grey polls of daws   generic these
peculiar   mine   to tree   bird   me   unique
as nursery nucule   that nought else would bear
but silver nutmeg   gold pear and   king's daughter

And pallid as sluiced veal   or rhubarb forced
this tom thumb   template   this more air than tree
assembly   vantage   hors d'oeuvres for
our doucest   sprucest   avian family
and   meagre mint for tanners and for guineas
      derision and absurdity apart
is   perpendicularly musing   prone
the same   for me beneath   philosopher's stone
mysterious mystical identity
of confine and escape   of shrink and stretch
like Alice   balancing hallucogens
of infinite   and infinitesimal
of iris thoughts   and shocks of sense   that flock
and nibble prettily   and pirouette
but never stand   on ceremony   still
presuming on their sibling privilege
in haste too rare   to stay with joy and grief
but hoist   me   too   in leafage incandescent
boosters that burn off   as they graze the sun
to pinpoint dazzle   flaring thence alone

Traveller's Joy / Old Man's Beard
Withy Wind / Virgin's Bower

"Traveller's joy"   said Gerard   for it decks
traveller's ways   and thinking   I suppose
of those broad liberal terms   of sheets on hedges
bleaching in spring   blankets in autumn   pinned
to air   a rare fosse of white breaths   or sky
to earth tresses   down plunging crow-stepped ridges
of trees   reaches of joy   to hold the eye
and yet not hobble feet   and even presage
between-sheets meetings   at the journey's end

And though the greenish and stubbed stars of June
blunt as June bugs   no whiter largesse have
than maybloom   meadowsweet   and offer less
yes   nothing   to a nose pressed close as bee's
a million harvest tedders   when they whirl
for curvilinear beauty   stand alone
no rose gall rivals   curling and crank-handled
like crinkling hair of comets   in old cuts
but trim and trig   held out on rigid stems
in radiating rightangles   like children's
windmills on sticks   No lines can complot more
to lift and spin the heart   not parallels
of finest machined graphs   or antennae
unscrambling galaxies   in a silver mile

And paradox unscrambles the last stage
        old man's beard virgin's bower   for hairline spokes
like spider's legs   fuzz into gossamer
yet keep distinction   and burr smooth   and only
in mass is mist   flossy but firm   to guard
dark raying hubs   deep as a sheep dog's eyes
behind grey tufts   like a cell nucleus
verging on fission   and these cornucopias
virgin but manifold   should be the bowers
blissful enough   to flag down travel   but
egg on the traveller to   ultimate joy.

Little Apple

Et *ego in* Arcadia

"Only in men's imagination does every truth find an effective
and undeniable existence." (Joseph Conrad)

So   there I was   at three   but unaware
momentous   as it was   to memory
and this felt more momentous counterpart
a life span later   that the anniversary
cum house warming   brought   yes   the comeliest
basket of plums   in all these years   but   more
that freedom of the place   all children share
but   most   investiture   still   only in
the emperor's new clothes   as infant king
of ancient orchards   in an impaired ring
of village   unique cornucopia
for common green   once seamless   but hacked through
in sorry parcels   by this looping grove
like continental drift   a sacrilege
to Pomona   midway on which   was I
hence   of the village   though closed book to me
smithy   and hall   and farm house   church
the inner ring   a barton and its stream
under the church   and quaintly called   the City
with villadom   its precincts   but this core
like sarsens   gapped survivors   of a cirque
bearing   plain   austere helpless   witness to
our villan usurpation   environing
the quartered fruitlands   and their ancient lords
Cheshire who beat his bounds at night   gun cocked
at fancied depredation   Leaper   the lame
and woodman Warrener   well stocked with ferrets
who left the artichokes   to choke his trees
and   The Carnarvon Arms   dreading the curse

Our bare crack had but two   a damoseen
and   massive hub   and axle   to the whole
smooth naked pollard   as that Aphrodite
with hieroglyphics   intricately scored
of arboreal tongues   so Adamic
its name is lost   a dendron Jupiter
struck   more than striking   with petrific bolts

To eyes less   closed   among the blind   philosophers
more blest   that festive basket   should have been
laid   votive   at its foot   as reverently
as for that boundless mark   and sacred tree
fruited with fluttering   aboriginal   awe

But   my awe   too belated for live fruitage
its occasion   too peculiar   to myself
to strike   other than peculiar   to others
but   upright   still   or prone   that fossil lives
in realisation   full   and clarified
gestalt   in vision   at this moment   always

Tree Fall – Epitaph

These autumn mornings   each both usual
and first   nothing asserts   or proves   or moves
not bird nor beast nor sap   nor sun   Here nature
selfportraits limns   in immobility
stirring the heart   more than herself   or art
a sum in grand addition   solved gestalt

Sun flows   regardless level through the boughs
and gladly choosing colours   here and there
to scatter extra through the lawns   "the light
that never was"   and always is   on autumn glades

This morning picks out its beloved faces
some favourite grace of limb   and   for each sitter
measures and fits a crisp cut suit of shade
remodelled by the hour   So   why   then   why
amidst the diamond tears of daily joy
these crimson flushes   sudden danger flashes   ?

Mark how the sun   with firm grave emphasis
distinguishes newcomers   to familiars
mourning ash mounds   whose fragile hoods hold all
their trees   like stars collapsed to pinheads   and
abutting massive butts   with target rings
of reds and whites still wet   cremations and
stones   in round counts   commemorating years
truer than bell or number   essences
that go with majesty and tragedy
themselves their symbols   present and evident
obviating mime and adumbration
of lapidary rhyme   Yet   to be launched
the epitaph   to tidy the rough wrench
what even sun and besom leave half staunched
or autumn crocus   moving in like nurses
protestant ministrants against the strokes

words must be agents   to complete   not end
the tragedy in nature's autograph
grander than Greek   through this engraver's stylus
still   but another craft   far other skill
          alas

"The Greatest Man That Ever Lived"

Since space and light do   most things   warp   or change
gears   since time does   or are annihilated
as in black holes this trinity   One thing
though it controls them all   does none of these
whether it appears   on this white page   or on
its unimaginable antipodes
of space   if soup enough goes round   to fill
so   round   the bowl $E=mc^2$

That first big bang was programmed   to pronounce
just that   for sure   and had it been as sure
in speech as act   and bellows at command
he might have been   not here to lip read it
clear short and plain   here on the tensest lap
and tip maybe   of gravity's elastic
before recoil accelerate to   or from
home point   or snap   Small choice he offered god
either to pop the paper bag   or hide
behind Big Bang   his fixed and inmost name
though elsewhere children elsewhen may reel off
for their first lessons   in a trillion schools
for all we know   what we know only nor
in unison   for half a century

Yet   in the file of pebbles on this shore
as full of numbers as the universe
amidst their colours   but and ben   that lurk
in air but live   in sea   I come to know to
nests of stone tables   not with coffee   grained
but glyphs   so worn so elegant   compulsive
to ciphering   what glosses can they be
but formulas   discarded   of creation
sequential drafts towards a final answer
tossed in the waves   as we still do   with tireless
and inexplicable   till now   addiction
as by a schoolboy   crumpling up his maths

or resubmission   for new synthesis
as into a computer   to return
rejected   through millennia   in shapes
of marvellous refinements   still unsolved
their only words   the scraping of the herds
till   something   scribbled on a single stone
and labelled   Albert   now   a hundred years
a ton up evolution   for a pebble
contained the combination that reveals
all   through expansion back to last contraction
though grist from that black mill   if it exist
worship withal for his uniqueness   may
call for a second thought   second equation
Anderer Stein   and what is this hushed shine
like characters brushed up a Chinese scene
that other stones   meandering the backwash
rush up to screen?

The Worm

As if the age were not enough: — easy
erasure of cities with a smudgy rubber,
hunger and holocaust and best intentions,
allies allied by interlocking hates,
uttering cross purposes or nothing,
but pre-fabricating for home consumption
millions of word palaces to conceal
(words are improbable waves but death quick on
the receiver draw at the distant end
is real enough though he never answer back)
despair, squat in the cellar, the sole content: —
each playboy in the world whips the same top
on a different axis: —
                              as if such times could not
like cold air squirting from the great fixed screw
of Gobi, or the bursting bomb, rack, draw
and quarter me by centrifuge, a worm
lodged in my intestines, wheels within wheels,
protects my own pain like a tariff wall,
deeper in defence than Ajax' seven-fold shield,
and clogs like oil at ease on thrown prone seas
the world's wild careen to a harmless reel
seen slipping off the screen in sleepy comfort —
but bolts my life staff whole like Aaron's rod.

Who gave me that worm? The godfathers and
godmothers of that age's dirty water,
or my prenatal pipeline or myself ?
— A placid happy worm biding its time,
kneading me from within as outside brasses
prolong the Siam neck, one ring a year
like trees: a worm with head well bedded in,
too lazy to turn on, grateful to, his host,
to whom he feels a brother or twin.

But like a sleeping cancer, an unnatural
baby that sprouts for ever in his sleep
till knocks not meant for his door wake him
and the door discloses his driving head,
my grim pet now, rationed in chyme, gnawed too
by odd short comings in stocktaking and
unaccountable jars from some god's machine
(a slight tote even when chance has synchronised it),
rouses like the Midgard Serpent on Doomsday,
but where he withdraws his newel from the house
this constricts me stricter to his fit, hisses
resign, resign, paps me with the poison
brewed from my own alimentary canal,
screws back my front to a horizontal plane,
my eye dull amber pupilled with a fly,
and see my forked tongue and pedestal tail.

Homunculus has come full circle, who
is here ?

Anchor Man (For Bevis)

The Venus Accroupie <u>on dit</u> once pig-
-a-backed a child   Could it be Cupid? but
the plaster martyr out there in the rain
by pain is doubled   not maternity
arms touched down to the earth   soon to reclaim it
patient to bear   not under starter's orders
with contoured locks made out in green the head
gravely inclined to tucked-in legs   amidst
the umbelliferae buoyantly rising

Though cast as first god in a maimed Olympus
the frequent birds use his convenient nob
as host and hoist taking both stock and stake
Round as her favourite curl the bobbing wren
curtesies herself into a hoop   then robin
red shield at rest his eyes fierce as a lance
mavis and dunnock on that willing poll
almost as light   as tits awaiting turns
to board the swinging gleaming dome above
of succulence that only they can ride
prone rods with drilling heads
                            Above whom still
dalliance of pigeons while   high roof to all
the starlings pitch a creaky umbrella

What juggling tiers balances that quiet nob
What shoulder above shoulder acrobatics
on that firm platform   downward as to pain
joyous   such towering happiness to bear.

The Secret Sharers

I share my tub   with some   unknown   (unknowns)
Towels   drip   gently   that were warm and dry
between   two visits   and there is a rim
round the clean bath   far better there   agreed
than lacing unknown necks   On whitest paint
claws   of minutest print   like eye black   round
and uselessly above   the handle   which
yields   it is true   to an advancing finger
but   disconcertingly   the window's steel
bursts open   only under force majeur
Runnels   smear mirrors   from untimely sources
and   comfortable noises   which may come
from ringing neighbour concerns   the night brings
or   closer   and more   intimately still   ?

As wishful party   to the   welcome beaming
from the pinned up   heater's rays   doubled indeed
were sight vouchsafed   of bodies conjured   only
from tracks and clues conjoined   like a child's puzzle
or   a polite veto   on the engaged door
or less forbearing word of mouth   I grant
since   beauty   drawing by a single hair
not mine   can err   that bareness   unprepared
by introduction   may elect to share
only its shyness   with my own   and so
by perforce choice   remain
                              your secret sharer   still

60

Moving
A Study In Yellow

Today I struck my friend at least his bones
at least   his ashes or   at most   his chest
bright prong rebounding   like a tuning fork
from where he should not be   When did he move
no change of address posted through the earth
like whale calls to   antipodean   kin
The rafters of his hipped and valleyed house
why did he leave   Was he ejected by
Rackmanite hoods pretexting unpaid rent
or by developers   as on the spine
of unappeasable young gowks   or shovelled
aside by workaholic moles   Ennui
over the unassimilating years
or colour preciosity   *That stupa*
planted above my head   is not the yellow
of my canary hose on that far day
     though Chinese tea rose petalled   poking out
like giant guy ropes   from that tiny tent
or flying crane or that cross grained   cross gartered
Illyrian steward   playing possum to
as unguessed guest   returning family
delighting clownage   pupillating to
a brimstone myth   commemorated here
by this Rosetta   bush for who can read
but rather have they run   it seems   apart
or bush or bones above ground or below
or both   historially   from clashing hues
or uncontentious continental drift
or mocker   of those slipping finger tips
of God and man in that high chapel roof
to cocking snooks   dear me   till brought up sharp
by bayonet at throat   or   cache detector
     and treasure trove indeed   but richer far
than metals minerals   flagons and torques

kings' helmets   blades   jewelled interments   Shall I
arrest   though slow the glacial runaway
unearth   to see what earth has made   of earth
"as men in China after an age's stay
do dig up porcelain where they buried clay"
        fortified ashes under siege to Thor's
engendering spittle   Even demigods
dear friend   or merely supermen   expose
thus would I not   to this polluted air
innocents at large to larger choice   of death
Water   earth   fire   and air   the lot   O   no
"Sleep on my love   better   in thy cold bed
better to be disquieted"   and I
shall disinter   not you   but your brier head
of hated tint   the most suspected urge
to emigration   to enrich you by
pergolas   nearer to your heart's desire
and keep your yellow   greener   in our hearts

The long and the short of it is ?

If you believe   as people will   for all
our knowledge says   that god has interest
though heaven knows why   still in humanity
then   not merely likely   but a certainty
        and John Muir does not lie   he used the face
the squared blank faces between heaven and earth
sheer from the black pit of Yosemite
as the language of his way of making things
Half Dome   Indians knew his jargon   *Tiss -*
- iac half dome   the other half   why yes
that glacier fancied   pocketed   as simply
as Muir his crust and teabag on his jaunts
and walked almost as timeless as these ents
serenely on   Cathedral Rock   his sketch
of the west fronts he hoped his men would build
and   Lord of all   El Capitan   the sheet
of foolscap   whose Mosaic tablet is
itself the entire mountain but evident
without inscription needed   master plane

And if   as some believe   cocking a snook
at contrary evidence   themselves accept
that every action   thought   and every feeling
every second from the cradle to the grave
of his trillions   he is watching   every one
then what more certain than   likelihood now
sheerly impossible   that on   this beach
this tiny cove   to match this tiny island
as exact parallel   he should have trained
his writing hand   the sea   to scroll the cliffs
boulders   shelves   pebbles   in clear miniscule
letters designs hieroglyphs   bestiary
freaks of his fancy   Lord's prayers on pinheads
angels' attendant dance   intaglios
of Sumer scenes softmoulded   glimmering   from
limbs   tapering back into   the seal   and coins

63

as old   and torques like curtain hooks   that preface
magic or message   Tara's harpless halls
the earliest lingua franca on the earth
shrew brain pans   of abandoned billows   scum
lace pricked on cushions   loofahs to scratch dolls
pages of Pugin notebook tracery
scales of iguanas   and their eyes   owl faces
hairnets round spice jars   on and on   and O
sea serpent flutings lithely linking all
over the ages   patient   humble   all
tentative formulas for the universe
down to a fingernail   as closely packed
as nuclear equations   and as prone
to error and blocked roads   but wrong so e'er
or eclaircissement   Archimedean
shall we not need   his patience   or maybe
all that he is to crack the codes and help
him out   but with such calligraphs   such art
please god   please man   why should we   save for fun
like Feynman   the wry joker   who is dead

To a Hedgesparrow

Slapped like a wet economy label
over the commemorative tablet
by unknown persons in the public garden,
obstructing the double barrels of her name –
her one lethal possession – you affix
a limp imprimatur only to her tail –
" – BERD ", itself a name homophonically
generically yours.   Dead birds you hob-
nob on a painted perch. And birds she lived
to save from hand and gun – the keeper's gun
the schoolboy's nesting hand – caught not red-barrelled
and hot-handed, but through invited words
in village schools and learned periodicals,
authenticated by research in woodlands
and, sole laboratory, her poky room.
For shining vessels on her dressing table
nondescript pellets in malodorous jars,
gnomic umbrellas once were full-sailed bats
before rolled tight in the stomach mill of the owl,
and other drabbled toilets of the kind –
of which her brushes were but larger growth –
except the gamechick's quills which keepers see
in every brown owl's bill along the sights
but she proved paranoia forestalis,
coaxing the gun to rest: herself the brownest
downiest owl of all, and stringiest crow
the brother whom she left her winged glades
to preserve from a widowed solitude
he hardly felt, on a fen so tame and kempt
its wildest waters were piped effluent.

But there with other silent searching fauna
like polecat erect or heron taking stand
in her fieldglasses' thermographic script
of roped and climbing runes she recorded
sedgewarblers' yellow lives from hatch to silence

(their first and last); until the farmer's witchwife
watcher intent as watcher, trundling from
behind the door's black slit along the dike
rings in a staggering hoop of twittery curses
the magic glasses that have spelled her lord
(ploughing abjectly) to outrageous passion –
a human farce less entertaining than
avian parallels in her serene glass.

But you she saved not by her gathering store
of unused observation underground
over the way there where the syllables
you obfuscate are cut into the stone:
and the plastering snow that hardened your compeers
of the great hedgerow, tougher far than you,
into stiff boards preserved you for a worse fate –
from winter's bleaching cramp to be unlocked
into the burning needles of the cat,
or striking relaxation of your neck
by her pet protege the owl, so that
you loll here helpless on her helpless name.

See now disposed on almost-bearing grass
almost restored, your neat nailscissor beak,
legs unretracting for the landing, eyes,
no eyes but quiet spots that were your eyes,
neck a sad ruff of light interior grey,
closed wings, tail debonair. In duck-egg bud
regarding you like streetlamps with bent heads
jonquils ring-fence you linking arms. I had
more to say to you, but your clever claim
to namesakes and this pretty garden's co-
commemoration misguided me to mine.
Sharing you should pardon, for though you died
on consecrated ground, though by the claws
she proved too innocent, it did lodge you
free and all found. Your posture called to mind
how, raddled neck awry, she played her games
of hand to knee to neck to head and such

tumbledown pastimes with the village women,
imagining instead inspecting grebes
through similar rituals with bits of reed. –
Her brother cricknecked too with dolorous tic
that, raised on his dry stalk above the rest,
at auction once knocked down a lacquered vase
almost his height, to him, and much less blank.

But why all this to do with them and you
odd birds, myself a dodo in the making,
and that unnatural preference for birds?
Not yesterday's absurds but that today
which has named scorpions its heir, I should
celebrate or denigrate, for scorpions
take radiation in the biggest dose, and those
of coarsest kind best cope. This sly unchartered
flight backward from the responsibility
of being for or counter the accomplished –
and the stern satisfaction either earns –
has no excuse except that scorpions
although the ultimate of evolution
are unknown here.

Three Uses of Cupressus Macrocarpa

Now   real estate   for lesser animals
is desperately   as for human kind
vertical   and   worse   prophetically
Space Ship   Cupressus Macrocarpa   aimed
up from the good earth all ready   at the stars
long colonising arrow   Noah's neo Ark

Steerage   though in the nose   a susurrus
of starlings   stacked up   like that ocean cabin
bursting with Marxes   and with half the crew
contented sweeper caste   for consolation
rehearsing gospel songs   too light to over —
— balance the show   too high for nuisance to
pigeons   burly constabulary   below
indifferent as Democritean deities
to keeping peace   amongst peace keeping doves
computerised   by income   and by colour
from gentle grey   to blatant nouveau riche
the idle singers   of an empty day
whose leit motif   the first awake selects
      as shut or open   decreed for that day
      windows   inexorably of earliest trams
a choice of love notes   only   though swift wings
dazzlingly white   do undertake patrols
of dreys of squirrels   unremarkably
grey   but   cynosure of neighbouring eyes
two all black beauties   pièces de résistance
who wear black offspring   round their necks like mufflers
bound higher than their longest pace   and lead
streakers   in fun and games   dodgems N times
accelerated   as on film   that put
small fry miscellaneous   out of joint
in skirts of hovercraft   that few trees own
preferring shins and toes   go bare go bare
ground staff gregarious   each its trade badge
of medieval colour   hopping ready
for the friendly pint

                        Whoever   over all
not without mayhem   sits at what controls
unknown but better viewed   though not without
Babel sideglances roundly   and not squeezed
as from a tube   by overcrowding   over-
spilling   on unfashionable quarters
second class citizens   waiting their turn
at the bird bath   towelling off   meekly
short of the fifth rung   of the garden gate
but with the procreant mass   of Melville's chimney
firm and unquestioned as the crowded tower
of boyhood comics Tiger Tim   I think
the name   beaming his penthouse window's breadth
each aperture below   a different snout
          Bruin and Brock   Jacko and Henny Penny
and fascination   which I later found
in Prescott's Andes   coloured as highly   by
his blindness   also with a different world
at each degree of height and heat   at base
bare Indian brave   to braver furs in cloud
and   seven miles high   the condor on plane wings

mission identical   but quarters   closer
a pair of crows flap over the hedge lazily
to their own supermarket   so close at hand
so many shelves   so variously stocked
and reach down   casually a special fancy

The Willow

John Heywood: Song of the Green Willow

Of this willow garland the burden seems small
But my break-neck burden I may it well call;
Like the sow of lead on my head it doth fall.
Break head, and break neck, back, bones, brain, heart and all.
All parts pressed in pieces.

Prelude Postscript

How now old willow sallow salix Sale's Butt
Past prime they say and what have you to say
That silver birch last of the sterling seven
you melted back is slow to be convinced
out canopied with neck ropes dangling yearly
nearer the drop and elm past prime indeed
yet reins back ever sharper on the lane
flinching contagiously to cars at risk
and ash's twin prongs panicking to flight
tear oppositely down their grey silk stale

Attila still of trees in Darwin's book
slight not the mutual aid that we all need
less meals on wheels drip feeds sing songs anonymous
than welcome presence from a sister city
to keep you young in deed

                Do not forget

assassinating on an inchmeal scale
makes Overbury's endless poisoning
an instant laser cut out in sci fi
rivals are also in a loyalty
equally chronic to a family
mightiest on mould   Titanic senators
in supreme sylvan courts Promethean
provision stores of all but fire for man
chambers of decompression night or day
defusing sunlight that would desiccate
or putrefy and water hole to hold
of complementing twins Flora and Fauna
two bright decks full   exploiters above all
of raw materials a planet's store
climate and atmosphere and minerals
a dishy crust to coach and to support

such perpendicularity   each ring
world gold   each breath of air a snack   Tycoons
whose limit is the sky   Carnegies   Morgans
so absolute they can be absolute
also   in benediction   round the earth
These are   you know   one with you   under the skin
you with star pin point redwoods   which the axe
rears   as it fells   to transcendental fanes
built in antilogy   of the new world

Superb Muir pent house   or suburban tent
you   whom we kill   at will   by magic carpet
tinctured with venom   or the close chain tooth
do make us possible   dear enemy
        just.

Down By The Sally Gardens

Slide hand and self between the skymop side
sweeping the earth of that testudo creeping
strataed in upright shocks and lateral faults
(Nature capsized)   like winter waterfalls
in Nippon prints   and bungalow facade
squat as the Nippon artists   and with luck
crook a lost traveller finger   at the bell
though foragers will follow through the door
like granted victors.

        This green avalanche
as near as V Day   and planted to that end
could mount not one   V sign — a golden sally
sans gold   sans weep   in soil lethal to willows
like Jack in the box's beanstalk overnight
swarmed up air shrouds apparent only by
the branch hung out to map and pennant each
stair above whipcord stair.
        There among others
bitter morello   lilac   greengage   pear
sumac laburnum   elm (even the elm
leaned out and backwards   and went thin on top,
danger   as great as landmark   to the street)
there died seven birches   silver alchemised
into that relentlessly projected jackpot
of golden boughs reaching   the lastest sally
or week end war   far out of ring a paw
over great apples   vegetable gold
as precious to this ragman on his rounds
as precious metal.
        This anniversary
turning on silver what for its golden left
save Roman solitudes?   Next meal the house
blessing already asked   a Lenten tidbit
temporary stopgap   in a too sweet tooth

for a comics monster with ten thousand mouths
in tune with the slow lurch.   What will the triffid
do   touch a tender trunk tip on it   lob it
underhand back   into the circling darkness
flick up the matchbox   onto hollowed shoulders
or sling it   high and hard   with a young gowk's
heaved irritation at unsib encroachment
at that high priest of treecults   on the gate   who
deserts outrageously his sacred grove
of All-trees   save the willow   the one tree
he cannot grow   to turn him every day
to mine   as to the East   as I do now:

> < Do not ingest us   pray   my name is yours
> by origin and schoolmates called me Sally.
> Like licensed station squatters underground
> safe sleepers in a war you scarcely knew
> instal us poor relations in your hall
>   my name can mean that too   Art de la Salle
> or on your fortieth storey   or so
> under the roof tree that your harpies ride. >

That hermit nurseryman's split open house
that   should have warned me   with his floor board bed
his one untended bed   that   and his death
behind my turning back   his last sale waving
my willow wand   farewell.   What greenwood god
fizzed in his hormone squirt?
                    Not that speck of a dwarf
eleven thousand up in S.W. California
where wrought iron bristle cones grow slow as metal:
four thousand years makes a pretty fine pine
and three feet tall pretty tall for a stripling
centennially seven   but three (I fear)
three inches   thick   prognosticates that rickets
may be declared   this age or next   a state
for every inch should pack a century
of vintage summers in a hundred rings.

In all creation   there   and only there
with bushy tails   off Highway 395
where bristle cones reclined on threadbare elbows
chainsmoke millennial cigars to ash

rare and far fetched as moonglass   one pinch enough
inside this graveyard belljar holdall   tilt

like a plastic dome to hive a city in
and deaden the forfended universe
to fix it in its tracks for nearly ever
as geese are set around a golden sliver
of willow stuck in the ground.

Two Way Sees Through

Coming at me from a different window
sun drains the sky to show me but a book
and silhouetted head of harder grey
on lit white wall. But in the other house
the engagement of the willow's frontier twigs
countlessly crossing each its neighbours like
the building China Wall three steps and back
baffles contains or splints light's raiding parties
to keep the colour treasures of the palace
unexcavated still: – as many blues
as frames to make distinct, from single silk
to main trunk thick. Where most is brunt absorbed
muster the coral cells, millions of lockets
a face in each all water colour all
mainly blue eyes paled by the warrior light,
freshening with size and impugnity of frame
to squares torques ovals of uncrackled blues
along the queen post galleries and stairs:
those central azures these that draw our depths
like craft as quick as light to find their own
in space of no recall: these pictures blank
to feed our feelings fullest beyond art
though squared my window onto that other house
that lattice, mirror of heart's bluest dark.

Willow Stay Bare

Willow stay bare and I no grudge will owe you
for the rare mixed grills and the dainty dishes
of bulbs that you and the squirrel betwixt you
scoff for your winter fare or fun, or poison,
from annual thousands dibbled close as pebbles
in antique squares and vandalised as oft
digits enlarging with your crinoline:
or your draughts declaring droughts as unremittent
over what you've left us of our broad acres,
and still uncoiling rootmops from the tub
you penetrate our drainpipes, swab them dry
like a pin a boy's mouth and a wild bird's egg.

Think of your loss behind funeral spring blinds:
think of your spectators' expectancy
beyond that curtain < for thine own safety >
– thy drabness too – steelslatted villain-proof
rebuffing even ticketed admission
to that million membered vertebration
(Gabo to whom's a baby's toy) of space
an occupation lateral coiled stair flighted
diagonal and perpendicular
criss crossed with energetic nodes of these
a varyingly uninterchangeable
blueprint of space in calibrations from
hairlines so fine only their shine defines them
to trunk Yggdrasil, newel that heaves the sky –
king post King's vault ziggurat igloo doms
stayed by their own stretched skin, whole architectures
only the globe or the imagination
could comprehend else in one family circle.

Populace of this designed occupancy
that uses each breathtaking cubic inch
as rightly as a child its drawing paper
and differently definitively defines it

is steady state or passenger or tourist
each from his proper storey of advantage
from pantile pigeon down to pantler robin,
treecreeper steeplejack dunnock the harrow
dive bomber merle his trigger-happy clatter
as automatic as his indignation
troglodyte wren whose modest Everest falls
short of the first string course in all but song
and on his quick funicular ascent
squirrel is king for even the cat looks
down and is lost, though tits perch topsy turvy
from bells swung by their icepicks as they peck
panels of Hansel and Grethel macaroon.

An ecology an architectonics
this then and more so many more interred
in the midnight of your termite monolith
as Beehive buildings in Sardinia
that only bronze lefthanded blades could enter
shapely as blank. Restless and hanging rolls
(only a god could hang them) of sodden paper
exclude my light and sight – a small loss ours
that knocks out passing cars or boys themselves
with stones kicked from the defaced drive defacing
the street's good name, but yours – Sir Orfeo's
self-glowing Hades in a hollow hill –
is like a Vermeer pilfered from a nation.
Air to inhale and eat you need and minerals
to mine but why like Rumour full of tongues
in billions and green lungs? Porphyria, mind
you do not torniquet your arterial trunk
with fichu crocheted in your own sharp cords
for ever fix you in your ochrine grace
as now no green about you save the moss
the weather pencils in as delicate shading
its Grenadiers infiltrating your van's
advancing self. – But so with < ever as now >:
already silkiest filaments are strutted
and tagged as yellow as forsythia

leaflets still curling tender from the press
to bill the black out shut down that will make you
invisible as a yak. Is the axe
or (Thor it must be) Mjolnar the right answer
– a death demanded to infrigorate
naked in his new suit the emperor:
template or image like the double helix
to show space what it has never seen – itself
down to the whorls that seal identity?

But would this crime, Asgard's in magnitude,
not serve to touch off Armageddon? Is
that wolf whistle from the leads the wolf himself
Fenris in dovedown straining on the collar:
Is Freyja's finger on the knob to keep
inclined so slenderly your golden lid
losing its hold? What is bold Robin saying?

Drown grounded tresses in green surging tears:
burgeon willow for fear of worse. Remain
still unobfuscate willow; reminder so
of more momentousness than guilty gods –
love's harmony of nakedness expressed
to the softest aspirate and lineament
and, because not to be deciphered or
descried or guessed from the disguise the bluff
the contradiction of the garb, a re-
velation like a throbbing galaxy
to tax the reverent the revelling eyes.
But since eclipse is all the world save me
should see who am refused even eclipse
on with and welcome your occlusion, willow.

Sing All A Green Willow Must Be My Garland

I. Winter Greens

Dusted this year as oak with lime the sallow
harsh desiccated canvas but though nature
half of herself her iron rain wind ball
swung from a winter derrick to jerk out
a nest of storeys like a chest of drawers
filtration proof as ever overlapping
zips of long leaves as shields themselves like wings
humped up or lunar kites leaning as one
down cockle shells in Senlac tapestry
or brush and quill, a million-rowed testudo;

but look where nonetheless the low down sun
like even the world's wealthiest boy has not
sneaked under rope and flap scot free to see
what circling troupes? No lions elephants
burst hoops and tiny tubs, no Aaron's rods
from flutes to snakes to their own airs turning
but first appearance in a solar turn
of the greatest raree show on any floor
quick change artiste your own sun's self a more
glittering gate crasher in one piece green gold,
golder than green a glow worm doorbell push,
than caverned amethyst in Atlas range.

Thirst parched the blades without within so patched
or sparse still less this glade's phosphoric hue
to gaunt big top arena's barren gloom
were due you'd say than name to Golders Green
and still be wrong for the perverse lamp shade
made to exclude not humanise the light
hugging abeyance like seraglio
yet on this sun spot pierglass dazzling
splashes the pent green essence it denied
not only to the world but worse itself

in every sense till mirror shows more true
than tree itself or so bright for a shadow
its object faded annihilated
and stayed instead.

    In an off colour season
that willow still can hatch and hutch a marvel
turn tabling usurpation of drained shade
to golden utterance of a green outlaw thought
as though a termite castle heavens high
where light means death should at the axle glow
into a revelation of its world
is marvellous.

II. Verdigris

The conjured circle in the sunset willow
as poet's license   or the flattest lie
who can deny   once seen   that green gold plat
that runs blood gold   but catches up the heart
short as those rarer buds   like bombs unhatching
of daffodils   lemon just leaving green
that doff distinction as they dip   to blow
into mere saffron   by the worm's eye sun
from fusty osier essence   to <u>green lion</u>
alchemically forced   despite the brown
holland dust sheeting   and caretaker's frown
and sulky keys   through the distended span
and summer of the unslaked watering can.

The miracles according to   Lo   I
the Man now winter murks preclude   with no
benefit of illusion   solar lasers
or a materialised spirit of willow
but if hands   sleeves are empty of all tricks
but a stick or two   for form's sake   or needs be
to mend the pace   whence those most moving greens

chasseurs verts   stridently that override
through thick and thin   wide arteries and city –
steeple – bye – and bridle – roads   stepped cattle trails
squirrel's brushed spike tracks   and the yaffle's drills
with dapper avian fleur de lys to crown
this tree   Peruvian dichotomy
from top to bottom so communicant
no foe surprises or   inside   escapes
green livery for a spring cleaning that steals
marches on spring? < Mosses on weather side >
but this fixed conference seat of cardinal rains
boasts no facade unstained   wherever   you look
there verdigris   the squirrel's contrary
is on that side   in green germane and true
to soak and submarine as grass and gire-sol
to the sun   illuminating limbs
bark rules and capitals   to chilling snakes.
Theatrical   sensational   and brushing
aside from notice   save as neatest foils
the close knit osier mail   whose winter self
is positive mellifluence   to revive
colour starvation   busy now   chainstitching
its own renewal   whence springs young Frankenstein
that outstrides nature   in such buskins   bred
in chemist's tube or head   in green room   or
preventive spume   from luminous cadaver
or cortic dry rot   or ?   Ask that almighty crutch
before its incommunicado   dark
self guarded aestivation   ask Old Crutch
that   three piled   shaggy   gaudy all with green
fons et origo stands   as equable
to aggro trouble on invaded pitches
by mufflered fans in Lincoln green as to
procreant cradles   endlessly rocking
or independent slips struck years ago
but neighbouring still   in windowpane and wind
manes   tossing   crossing   tenderly   slenderly
in instant birds nests   and unmade in less.

Not Proven *or* Still O The Will O

Into thin air   from sleep guilt surfacing
that changes all   with wonder   to find all changed.
From dream still projects guilt   like this armchair
that plankwise tilts   twixt edge of back and seat
myself   who must not   rising send it flying
on fast accelerating castors   back
from house arrest relieved   until the die
to enforce verse   or to first square reverse
on the gamesway   is cast.

      On what   though   always
on what   on what but on this same   all change
for   inside sleep   autumn has hounded out
brown pelted flocks   that browsed and clothed the sky
and streamed them down the alphabet to earth
in airy syllables of record time.

From parted thus curtains   and unlit fauteuils
what scaena opens   upon opening eyes –
a crystal palace   echoing glades between
– blacked out by war's decades   a colosseum's
first floodlit silenced second – archery
of osiers   shafts reglancing to the ground
only for lacked neck room   caryatids
with heads that need no hod   to carry skies
though oaks   in turn   seem to wear osier yokes
all native aspiration   Afro styled
corkscrewing reinforced steel oil drills   still
by rhythms fathoming and plummeting
    contained   reversed   skeletal gamps.
        And as this
dilating medusoid   this dear enemy
in slow conducive   undulating passes
metamorphoses into one   itself
all within ball and sceptre   so this lamp

red into sulphur disc   usurps the cloak
or shadow   of the abdicating sun
that sun abandoned   slabbed and yellowed shale
that incombustibly defeated fire
while   worlds below   the willow's lagging hem
delicately unpleating and repleating
is gemmed with sparkles   neutralised and civil
of far off traffic aggro   unique bonus
like rarest particles   extinct as born
but realised   identified   and sprinkled
by time impossibly upon a screen.

Centrally fixed in cooling courts of the sun
the batten spreads gold fleeces for footstools
or overtakes leaf flight with sent on treasure
belated gold hand shakes   as Antony
Ahenobarbus did.
                   Barbaric glow
so mescalins boards to let   but when the Act
when does the poem begin   with   Gentles   here
come I   Beelzebub   with broom   or my
almighty club   but come to clear not fill
a room.   What Turkish Knight   or hobby horse
or comic resurrectionist   the bill
will fill   or foot   if all creation fail
or circling in John Henry's leaking pail
are we   in water drops too sparse to make
a teacup maelstrom   an uplifting fate.

Poem delaying   still   apologetic
the chairman   left to hold the fortress   spreads
his filibuster preface thin and thinner –
Since often images may best reveal
and in a deeply different light   the case
from consciousness' state of speciousness
and so theatrical the imagery
if show   and being other   is to be
the real right thing   what else than double falseness
can content have to show a doubleted

or buskined presentation of the present
in language   tailored   gestured   and much larger
than life   now   or when words were longer yet
than life   pin points that jetted trails of vapour
to score the sky.

       And may the gargoyle fade out
some warble   cadence   meaningful or – less
in either case incomprehensible
such as moved Beckett's   Mouth   and all its lovers
a play without a play   but not without
a theatre   a clock   and a box office
by its own plight to simulate the might
    schemers   pretenders   young and old apart
the now impossibility of art
to become art   for its or any sake
not be the admission to sincerity
closest   that closest makes and meets   my case
or screaming   such as that   inaudible
in Munch   in Bacon   and in Bevis   but
also invisible   though my strong suit is
also with others   that we both are wrong.

No Numbers Please

Half gone   thirds gone   fractions   what can they tell
of scale   of majesty   spiders have scale
can lose a sixth   wrap up a bug with five
atoms and galaxies   inside and out
have number enough   to be numberless
after such amputation   let us say
rather   like close up   heavy weights   your stubs
still jab straights   rounds   uppercuts enough
into the January   evening sky
cleaned up   not out   not counted out   just stunned
empire   decolonised   but dominioned still

And spring will sprout   green unversal down
like glistening hairs   on Harry Ploughman's arms
but pristine and surprised   and now you draw
the grey heaven into you for coverlet
leaded   nine B   or graphite   or charcoal
but let there be no mistake   and you be
tree   basic   minimal   abstract of   tree
the artist   culling you includes   held out
Yosemite   waterfalls   of tresses like
Rapunzel   for the climbing eye delicate
to invisibility   like the H
highest of seven   of the tortoise hand
crawling across the page of   Bryan Pearce
to peering tourists   imperceptible
puzzled in St Ives   pencilling a sheet
to leave it blank   as with your own white wounds
no numbers should   disfigure those dart boards
contoured already   with gyring designs
but uncompetitive   with beech or ash

patent the sacrilege   but so the shape
of things to come   spaciously intervalled
innocent   now   against all violation
of water   laws   from deadly piping roots

intruding unsolicited supports
to footings   dense   as counterparts *ci-devant*
draining occluding clouds   for which you bled

So let us   contemplate   rejuvenation
from waste   fertility   your own untwined
surcharged   like Daniel Lambert's embonpoint
who only sat   from monitors triennial
to death by numbers   cost effectiveness
from ABCs or *arbor economicus*
requiring the death penalty   themselves
by the monstrosity of increment
that they condemn   condemned

             Negative these
that darken with the night   but necessary
like antimatter   that unseen   vertebrate
sine qua non   but here   is positivity
itself   massive diagonal across
the vulnerable pane   its nobs   like pegs
for a gods' hat stand   with soon its own Robin
Hoods shakos bows   and   look   where   even   now
one trig log   upright   on the barren hearth
to glad the eye   by beauty   not by glede
hangs   out   three pennants of identity
indelible   as Brighton rock   as setting out
to keep green   memories   in rootless   sap
of that gaunt   gianthood   its source   Tom Thumb
yet taller than its sire   in shared defiance
of fate   What number   whole divisible
infinite   not high powered singular
negative   splintered   can be fitly seen
in company with   immeasurable   these.

Absalom My Son Absalom

To think spring sunsheened filigree should ever
be silk Rapunzel crop   to revelation
of massive tangled corrugated trunks
gamp Cyclopean   Asgardian majesty
for all its mere half century of life
between two sons   third son   or desired daughter
she calls you whimsically   hair no clue
unisex days and   even Roman trees
were female   despite masculine declension

  Decimation that would stun a Rip Van Winkle
back from nonage   though moraine still diffuses
moiety shock as from a glacier grinding
to smoothness   sites and sights   for humankind
or shearing plane that shapes such cabinets
  what cruelty or necessity required it?

Fertility   that wastes manges deranges
hen runs and folk   or beauty parlour cull
in deference to your variegated fame
from China to Peru? Or say you are
like other beauties better known   addicted
a demon for drink that would skin a stone
and drives you underneath suspect foundations
to drain them   dry and dropped   so   to reverse
dry out yourself   you must be denuded
defrocked and not quite drawn and quartered
feet foiled   against a subterranean baulk
like rosebud toes once mandarined from beauty
or autumn floods   fraying against adamant?
Whatever cause   and captive your acceptance
must be   hers so   relievedly happy
for temperate escape from filicide
and by an unanticipated beauty
justified in the event   like Maggie's strike
of locks about her   black as her mood that time

glossed into dazzling grace. How unreserved
can pardon be   with accessibility
so new externalised   like Pompidou
from dome   to loaded left   shifted in list
à la Nippon   like too   in best from least
but in light perpendicularity
        mullions and slits a million burnished blades
        the blue set in innumerable leads
itself a heaven   like heaven   a mystery
extinct   some say   British from top to toe.
Your elder brother gains his half century
with loss of more than half his canopy
as you   but his is irreversible
Tertius is overweight   but you are scaled
as jealously as a boxer at weigh in
moreover   signatured   to sweat more off
under requirement   of the cyclic year
or grooming for a model on the catwalk
but undisturbed reaction   pro and con
dating from days when   with a negligent hand
they bowed the tree now compounds the offence
lese to the majesty that hedges you
sustaining   leaning towers   or Rufus pinned
red as his name against his father's oak
Absalom hanged by hanging from his mane
Samson in training behind strengthening bars
and   once   a cross

        Intervention of my own
in family divergence   cool and warm
proposes objectivity   and history
to see you as a gowk that dodged the draft
awol   when conscripts left for Africa
and under ceaseless undivided care
became the monster habit never noticed
mottled gladrags   innocent of moulting
to sober grey   turkey to hawk   your mass
and height in winter threatened safety   ours

your own worse circumambulents'   top heavy
to flinging summer rain and to my fears
but now   winds whistling thorough   spaciously
whistle for me too

        So much for judgements
of praise and blame and balances   which leave
unspoken all that matters   but how can
words like devalued banknotes in cartloads
or coins used into anonymity
work miracles save that shaven and shorn
or maiden half forlorn towering between
you   stand even   with your siblings   all in all

(At the suggestion of Penelope Sale)

Final Demand

The weeks   taught us elegance   how   on ice
in padded tuns to fall   Weeks then of wind fall
breaking sound barriers   amidst the rest
catching up April   and her louchest showers
in one contemptuous swig   into the Eagre

My prize arrived   post haste   and barring exit
great willow bough   its note   to my address
Thousands to be won   and the next will come
registered post   dissent truncated

Willow

mother of millions   peering up   O willow
into your condominion of the air
space circling station   never before
Sale versus Salix   alias Frankensteins
never   in all our flytings   have I seen
you   as star warrior   threat   but rather as

sparring apart   a bean stalk world of wonder
poor Jack   my eye   and privileged to wander
radiant arteries   at bewildered will
triumphal   engineered   dichotomy
oriels   and oubliettes   and Mars canals
yet outmost curtains   hair line   fountain drift
mobiles   dictated by   softest suggestion
but now   you write   fell as a Rackham wood
nidification   true   is all your own
and birds   though multidecked   passengers only
Absorber   yes   and adding widening whorls
to whorls   like budding snails   or weighing weights
common by common   surrounded and enclosed
below   and regular high jinks above
architectonic antics   in big top
Paxtons   though regularity itself

would cheer   like kids   But this dropped portcullis
declares a new dimension of intent
from iron curtain   until now bamboo
bombing   in saturation   or attrition

See you   as that reared hard ware   in the sky
I must   that must descend   a thrashing whale
larger than any thing that ever lived
dinosaurs for flippers   diminuendo
even capillaries   are men of war
given our nearness   a destined   some time end
to both   and   so   our farewell verse of willow
that you cannot desire   much   worse than I.

Towards Amends

Say I have ever taken your name in vain
or called you impudent or horseplay names
misnomered lower branches of the clan
makers of baskets or of cricket bats
or of my cockney self   or so I claimed
exploding bloodsucker   or buccaneer
of the year   or century   or of all time
triffid   rogue elephant   or such fantastics
as pylons subjugating soils and selves
demi- though domesticated early
in the pigmied tribes   thalidomidal ogres
bestriding the engirdled earth   do not
despite accordance with desert   do not
answer me in that same despiteful kind
that would demean yourself as much as I
or me but as behind you the night tightens
on poles of light and black the blue that you
into your coopered continent   inhale
as ash sucks yellow from the sunken sun
or beeshanks pollen   but exhale also
more royal and confirmed   your head the sky's
your pale flanks substitutes on touchline benches
– as night draws on   and out   and sees enforced
gives heightened colour to your majesty
and awe unanswerable as you its own
from that unfinished height   your frame receded
or overshouldered like the gates of Gaza
eye and great window now a telescope
that gaze directed for one terrible moment
from looming grandeur towards recognition
that concentrated presence bent upon me
collected from root bole branch grounded hair
impenetrable to question   and the need
to sentence or forgive   unthinkable –
and I am answered   though no longer there.

Willow Pattern

To Penelope

Two   images   compose in her   awake
and not the filmy un projectability
of dream   but kicking and alive   one   willow
and clear   but   suggestive   of chinoiserie
two   bridge   a goal curled   at the burrowed heart
pencilled by David Jones   that saw me safely
and sane across   war's   Piranesian   prisons
vertiginous no go   vortices   some kind
          the sallow   of a baton   handed   planted
on   V Day   of a peace   no less insane
taking off   cauchemar   itself for heaven
letting down silkstrong filaments   to climb
into the perils   of a beanstalk world
or to disclose the Land of Looking Glass

monopolies   of my verses   manshaped   one
proportions   correspondent   beauties   business
in gestes and gene   the other   Cyclopean
aggressive symmetry   if peace   a Roman
powered to push the sky   and us   whom it
yet loves   from house and home   even though branded
for safety sake   the one   a pictured bishop
cathedral in his hand   the other   that
chalk giant   pole in hand   motivation
notionally   both   to the same end
but   by Minerva's   unaccountability
to-ing and fro-ing   with the lessening oars
and all the perverse ingenuity
of Tom   her demon son   delivering
so grievously   poor Jim   already free

presented   beggarly   to Penelope
to solve disjunctions   oracularously
or mirror images   rocked on the stream

who   cunning   in nocturnal   erasure
of daily incompatibles   conversely
intuiting   the hidden   yin and yang
in arches   quick and stone   dear osteopath
bone into   socket   clicking   homecoming
like Lily Briscoe's esemplastic vision
envelopes them within a harmony
whose comfortable   majesty engenders
a symbiotic congruence   while on
her black box loom   she weaves   the willow pattern

Notes

The Bridge

The Bridge in Motion

moving: without "that willing suspension of disbelief . . . that constitutes poetic faith" (S.T. Coleridge), the maniform reflections of the sun lit water on the various faces of the bridge

fairings: a thin slip of closed lattice with a feathery head that shoots out disconcertingly when pressed at the other end: a toy

cakewalk: another feature of the fairground, of rudimentary entertainment and, so, probably obsolete, consisting of a long platform that moves forwards and backwards in jerks that make walking deliberately difficult

Bridge Accosted

Mickey's crew: free of the laws of gravity and other such risible simplifications

Fougasse: a wartime hoardings artist

steel: bridges

yardstick's: the standard use for objects of that shape is now a stick of bombs

Bridge Arrested

springy arthritis: paradox suggested by the stubbed but vital appearance of beech twigs

pontic arms: one of a number of panels of shallow reliefs on the four sides of the bridge

palace: of the Sleeping Beauty

idolon:	deceptively attractive generalisation
harrowed . . . end:	prophecies of doom speak to one somewhere deeper than the intellect's rejection of them

Second Anniversary

secret:	the atom bomb
timber claws:	trees uprooted and swept down by the current
the difference:	between my old view of the gracious bridge and the sudden vision, seen from the other bank and the opposite directions of the imperfect and less sensitive old prints, of its angular disjunctiveness as the reality; unfair, but a useful projection of my post atom bomb disillusion
bomb:	disillusion
lymph:	v. the end of 'The Bridge in Motion'
impermanence:	the end of the war (and after) left a vacuum, a feeling of unreality; solidity was destroyed by the explosions and those soldiers' yarns of visible shadow replicas of the absent buildings
autarkic:	self sufficient and proportionate

Third Anniversary

Tahitian prow:	an aesthetic and peaceful contrast to the tree battering rams of the previous anniversary. But the cubist style reflections of the bankside trees do reveal the current despite the sun's temporary absence
lank chapels jaw:	Unforgivably unfair but Austerity survived the war and the spectacle of the chapel unlighted by its stained glass, its surfaces streaming with cleansing water and its vacuum accentuated

by *cap a pe* Piranesi-like scaffolding did contrast sadly with the small bright intact bridge, a natural survivor

candour: A research student was writing his thesis entirely on the many 17c connotations of the word 'candour' but did not live to complete it

Wren's bridge's: Trinity bridge is next to Clare and although not distant in time its correspondent features very heavily and pointedly indicate the difference between the two Caroline periods. (A contentious attribution of the pontifex of 'Wren's' bridge to the son of him of Clare (Grumbold) makes the change the more glaring.)

Bridge Rebuilding

hound: a superb Dalmation that redeemed its commerical

line of beauty: Hogarth wrote a treatise on this necessity

nearly eight: four legs at speed seem double

salt water: buoys fish and oars boats

keystones slipping: the undulation was commonly, but wrongly, attributed to sagging

flamingo croquet: the kind Alice found herself playing

Arion . . . acorns: The etiolate relief on one of the panels with its "Unnatural natural history" is contemptuously contrasted with medieval correspondents: here, with the famous pigs in the chapter house of Southwell Cathedral stretching up to pluck the stone acorns, but undiscoverable on request, by dean if not by chapter, on my last visit

Miscellaneous Poems

A Horizontal Afternoon

From a sequence on the siestal role of afternoons

for general   unopposed inertia becomes the total paralysis
strikes . . . crazed: which is the last phase of syphilis

Noah Stylites

Second Flood: WW2, which later encroaches on, and isolates, him

roric: dewy

mud geysir . . .   German fascism attracted much attention over
fascination: here

fowl: I had 'hen', which was ambiguous

(as they   There was an upright rabbit ('rodents') warren,
will comb . . .   a springy cattle-bean stack, on one of our
skyscraper):   walks – a strange sight

cracks: The plaster of the new house contracted
slightly as it dried out, causing such minute
patterning of stress lines as seemed
themselves to constitute the walls

Melville: While on his return from whaling, Melville
enlisted on a U.S. man of war, but too late for
the regulation issue of uniform and bunker. To
meet Cape Horn weather he contrived a
padded garment from an old shirt, which, when
he fell from the main-top, threatened, in the
absence of waterproofing, to drown him – a
failed test of attempted autarky

The Mist

As the infinite series . . . nerve is numbed:	To try to render an un-broken continuity of dream and awaking which the morning mist seemingly affords, use is made of A level maths: the sum (e.g.) of 1 plus 1/2 plus 1/4 plus 1/8 . . . approaches, but never reaches, 2
Relief . . . never left:	Continuity of the signature is not broken by the window: the mist sustains its suction into its own indeterminacy, from which, at some unknown point, it returns and continues its upward flourish unbroken: too fanciful for comfort
Balshazzar's:	The writing on the wall that predicted his doom
crib of neurosis:	Ideally, in Freudian psychoanalysis, knowing that an obsession is due to a now-recalled incident in childhood is the combination that unlocks the safe of recovery
reticulate . . . decoy in:	The net and decoy bird that lures down and traps (gin) a passing flock of birds which are, in this case, appositely seen as bate (pipistrell)

A Transformation Scene

A probably tangential number from a failed sequence ('Heartborn'), in which elected stoicism is challenged by fatherhood

Euhoe:	pagan and short (by a syllable) for 'I am possessed'

'I must devise'

I inspiring . . . meat:	Pain is not a mere parasite but has taken me over, lock stock and barrel, and I am only the witch's executive (familiar) – an inversion role so complete that it strengthens and somehow satisfies

105

'The Universal' or Popular Science

vacuum machine: black hole in space

mages: astronomers

mentors: astronomers

answers . . .
accounts: The facts are right though theories change

Oberon the yob: Pluto, god of the underworld, became the Oberon of folklore

scales: of measurement

crane fly: Wasps eat daddylonglegs systematically

black cul de sac: womb

time . . . tumble: Time seems unimportant in some modern theories, serving as no more than brackets round an algebraic term

svelte warded: polished

the latest cry: I have forgotten to what these dernier cri proliferations refer – apparently of good omen.

Haydon: Benjamin Robert: a bad painter who kept a good journal with many reminiscences of the Romantics

The Tree

rammle: rubbish

galt: stiff clay soil which holds water (lakes)

High Jinx

might have been a kind of trailer overbalancingly tagged on to the skirts of the Willow sequence (q.v.) until the poem declared its theme to be about the colonists rather than their (temporary) colonial territory (and the abandoned Palace did stink)

three years . . . **shower:**	"The Education of Lucy" (Wordsworth)
furious . . . gut:	Sir Giles Overreach to his servile lawyer, Greedy: " . . . there is a Fury in that gut"
Asgard:	As the dwarves building the palace of the Norse gods felt they were underpaid, they were careful to make it not to last too long (the first cowboy builders)
Steinberg:	an artist wedded to disconcerting brinkmanship
After London:	Richard Jefferies envisaged London as a forerun Hiroshima, with buildings that powdered under the touch of a treasure hunter, roofed by a nuclear cloud
gridded carriage:	without the networks of bearing twigs that enable nests
Eamonn Duffy:	an ebullient don, whom I owe

Tit Chat

The solitary bird that stays unusually long and still looking at him is
interpreted as a greeting from a distant fellow fancier. He is
reminded of a visiting kit that preluded the war when nightingales
drowned the sirens

coconut:	half at a time

Accidental Voices

radio-active voice:	the dawn 'chorus' that may be inspiring the rest of the world, for all he knows
screwed leaf:	poem itself and bed – pathetic alternatives to the vanishing eclipse of reality

Art and Algy

Metronome . . . wrong:	scientists who would love to give their theory a push, fatally in this case of the proverbial stargazer who fell in the ditch
Darwin:	model scientist who left his sickbed and braved the storm to observe the coiled bryony tendrils that withstood its force
counterpart:	infinitesimal particles that can be equally explosive
keeps for ever . . . brain to hand:	Inside the atom yields secrets that may begin as mental concepts
quod . . . quia:	One method of proof was by disproof of other possibilities: now absurdity is used as proof ('<u>because</u> absurd')
riddles:	a games way to present fundamentals
nothing upon nothing:	as in the calculus
tramper's pebble:	In the folktale and Yeats's play, the pebble produces soup from clear water by the 'magic' of elicited additives
aggregates:	as in infinite series
right:	straight
Schlemihl:	ancestor of Peter Pan
<u>imprimatur</u>:	Catholic permission to publish

Nettles

Struwwelpeter's ungulance:	lifelong untrimmed nails of Shockheaded Peter, the naughty boy of a German book of cautionary tales

long S . . . Bath:	end patterns on the rods that straighten bulging walls; a Gorgon's Head discovered in Bath: also thought to be the Persian sun god

Fostered Alike . . .

Nature educated Wordsworth through both its beauty and its moral lectures ('Prelude', Bk2)

harvesters . . . bread:	The combine harvester is imagined as completing its dealings with wheat by delivering bread
blenching:	Indian scientists believed that plants shrank from human contact, proximity, even
March . . . origin:	Later experiences of natural beauty have not diminished that first shock, which has been refined and polished by time
ideal . . . other world:	'the idealising effect of twilight' (S.T. Coleridge)
first remembered:	The other 'first' – the invitation – may have helped the experience of beauty

Birch Hats

Harpo's . . . sticklebacks:	Harpo Marx well equipped as a dogstealer ('Horse Feathers')
angle:	fishing rod
spray:	scattered bait? otherwise, like fish eggs, leaves
black sheep or troll:	too heavy, possibly by malice prepense
Noel pane:	coloured lightbulbs on the window Christmas tree

Sparrows . . . flutes:	Sparrows cannot bear to watch the feasting, but whatever it is the birch has to offer they cannot discover any more than when fruitlessly imitating a bullfinch buoyantly deseeding a thistle
bare boles . . . blanched:	v 'Little Apple'
meagre . . . guineas:	Tundra trees are sparsely leaved, here in silver and gold
philosopher's stone:	alchemist's gold elixir
iris:	rainbow
flaring thence alone:	thoughts etc. passing the sun into space, as Hyperion did in Keats

Traveller's Joy

The alternative titles in Gerard's Tudor herbal may be regional, as in Geoffrey Grigson's 'The Englishman's Flora'

crow-stepped ridges:	Crows are here given the role of cattle wearing horizontal tracks on hillsides

Little Apple

common:	usually a green but in this case an orchard
Pomona:	apple goddess
closed book:	significance not realised
the curse:	Tutankhamen's supposed curse on tomb robbers, one of whom was the Earl of Carnarvon, chief landowner in the village, which wondered how far the curse reached and seemed to have survived

to eyes . . . blest:	To Wordsworth a child was an eye among the blind, a blessed philosopher ('Intimations' ode)
sacred tree:	in Africa, hung with votive tablets for fruit
gestalt:	in a flash

Tree Fall – Epitaph

'the light that never was on sea or land'	(Wordsworth)
fragile hoods:	the outer layer of ash
stones:	Rings in the cross sections record age like gravestones
bell or number:	funeral bell tolling the age of the deceased

'The Greatest Man that Ever Lived'

soup:	soup made from debris that fills (as far as is known) interstellar space
tensest lap . . . snap:	As the universe may have reached maximum expansion, it may be about to contract
inmost name:	too awful to be pronounced
scraping of the herds:	'melancholy long withdrawing roar' (M. Arnold: 'Dover Beach')
black mill:	What emerges from a black hole would have its own laws
Anderer Stein:	second stone to Einstein's one; this prophesy has been fulfilled

The Worm

Aaron's rod:	swallowed up rival rods / snakes in one gulp
the Siam neck:	(female) would collapse if its yearly rings were removed

Anchor Man (for Bevis)

Venue Accroupie:	(Crouching Venus) a sculpture in the Louvre
dome:	half coconut

Moving

house:	rosebush roots
Rackmanite . . . rent:	particularised term for the practice of forcible evictions
stupa:	poor man's pyramid (S. American)
Illyrian steward:	(*Twelfth Night*) Malvolio
Rosetta:	not (primarily) tautology but a stone the hieroglyphs on which once 'read' revealed ancient Egypt
historially:	memorably
chapel:	the Vatican, on the ceiling of which M. Angelo painted God reluctantly parting from Adam, his latest fad
'as men . . . clay':	Donne's version of a 'chestnut'
Fortified ashes . . . spittle:	Thor also made man, more specifically by spitting on dust thus 'fortified' as sweet sherry is by brandy
'Sleep on . . . disquieted':	a misquote from Henry King's elegy on his wife

The long and the short of it is   ?

ents:	pristine giants
Lord's . . . pinheads:	perverted miniscularity
Sumer:	earliest known city
Tara's. halls:	Irish excavations (New Grange): cf Tom Moore's song, 'The harp that once through Tara's halls,' etc.
Pugin . . . tracery:	delicately intricate designs by the Gothic revivalist
blocked roads:	investigations that lead nowhere
Feynman . . . dead:	cf <u>The Wife of Bath's Tale</u>: 'No man but Lancelot and he is dead'; a nuclear scientist who set himself problems for fun and played practical jokes on Los Alamos colleagues

To a Hedgesparrow

name:	Hibberd-Ware
pellets:	irreducible remains ejected through the beak
gamechick's . . . to rest:	She proved brown owls innocent of the crime of eating young pheasants by examining their pellets
paranoia forestalis:	'wood (mad) in this wood' (A *Midsummer Night's Dream*)
thermographic . . . runes:	movements of her binoculars
the farmer's witchwife:	believes she is stalking her husband as he ploughs

games:	Again, ruefully dutiful parochial occasions were lightened by comparisons with avian body-language rituals
tic:	which was taken as a bid

Three Uses of Cupressus Macrocarpa

Marxes:	in A Night at the Opera
idle singers . . . day:	borrowed from a poem by William Morris (except for the plural)
shut . . . trams:	When there were trams the degree of openness of their windows was fixed by daily decree from somewhere above
all-black beauties:	squirrels – a very rare and unsolicited honour for the tree
out of joint:	The novelty of the black beauties distracts due attention from the beauties of the small birds in the ground level quarter
medieval colour:	Trade and class had their compulsorily distinctive colours
unfashionable quarters:	spill over into a small-brother conifer suburb
chimney:	of which the massive strength promised safety and its warmth fecundity (I and My Chimney by Herman Melville); the syntax is 'but is better viewed roundly with the procreant mass . . .'
Prescott's:	Conquest of Peru, a narrative by the purblind American historian, which distinguishes the way climate and altitude create different societies up the Andes
supermarket:	<u>cupressus macrocarpa</u>

Willow

Prelude Postscript

**ash's twin
prongs . . . stale:** an execution at which I was dangerously
present

sister city: a neighbouring willow: actually a daughter:
symbiosis is hovering somewhere in the air

Overbury's: a layabout member of "the mob of (17c)
gentlemen who wrote with ease." In this case
his poetic facility landed him in the Tower,
whence his enemies poisoned him gradually
with equal ease despite his loud protests to an
unheeding world

Titanic senators: Keats's defeated Titans ('Fall of Hyperion')
strewn about like felled majestic trees

Muir: John Muir, the U.S. conservationist, who ran up
every sequoia in Yosemite

Magic carpet: acid rain

Down by the Sally Gardens

testudo: the Roman armies overcame all opposition by
locking shields and advancing with the
deliberation of a tortoise

week end war: the Israeli lightning strike against Egypt in the
1960s

Roman solitudes: "(Rome) makes a desert and calls it peace"
(Tacitus)

**a young
gowk's . . . :** a young cuckoo is usefully provided with an
irritable backbone which enables him to shrug
overboard the legitimate nestlings

115

slow as metal: I read somewhere that metals expand with the years

plastic dome . . . : R. Buckminster Fuller wished to do this; also, a millennial project for London

geese: are said to identify their herdman (or girl) with his stick and will stay by that in his absence

Two Way Sees Through

the other house: the willow, which does all kinds of wonderful things with light, in contrast to the steady dull silhouette of the observer in his house. With hindsight there may be a flavour of Henry James's spooky *The other House* (originally a play)

palace: Egypt Valley of Kings

Willow Stay Bare

Gabo: Russian symmetrical sculptor

loss: like an old master locked away in a vault

Yggdrasil: the tree in Norse mythology which holds the world entwined

harrow: a pair of hedgesparrows drag a lawn for food like the tines of a harrow, none of which plough the same furrow

Sir Orfeo's: in the medieval romance poem, Orpheus disappears into a hill and finds himself in a wall-lighted paradise

Rumour . . . tongues: which is how he appears in 2 *Henry* IV

Porphyria:	Porphyria's lover strangles her to perpetuate the height of their ecstasy in Browning's poem of that name
yak:	whose physiognomy is hidden in its woollen blanket
Mjolnar:	Thor's hammer
Fenris:	the world wolf imagined as a kind of steel hand in a velvet glove, or Red Ridinghood's pretend grandmother
Freyja's:	Thor's wife's
unobfuscate:	obfusc is ceremonial dress
save me:	I cannot now think why: clearly some extraneous exasperation meant to balance the preceding 'O altitudo'

Sing All A Green Willow Must Be My Garland

I. Winter Greens

zips . . . tapestry:	an invading boat in the Bayeux tapestry
seraglio:	the hareme is forbidden territory

II. Verdigris

green lion:	a stage in the process of alchemic projection
brown . . . sulky keys:	furniture was covered up in mansions shut up for the summer, unpropitiously for visitors
Lo I the Man:	epic evocation
chasseurs verts:	French cavalry regiment
Peruvian dichotomy:	serial dividing into smaller units, as in Peruvian (or Venetian) constitutional structure

squirrels contrary: a climbing squirrel will sequentially put the tree trunk between itself and too-close inspection

winter self . . . starvation: willow's green stands out as a positive in winter, though unnoticed in more colourful times

aggro . . . Lincoln green: Greenpeace activists dug up cricket pitches

independent slips . . . wind daughter willows, though freestanding, are very much in view

Not Proven or Still O The Will O

alphabet: leaves seen as letters ready for use by the poet?

first floodlit silenced second: breathtaking end of blackout: birth of a poem?

oaks . . . gamps: even with hindsight I cannot make out what an oak, seen as both contrast and lookalike to the willow, and with apparently futile augurs as branches, has to do with this poetic foreplay, but the process is apt to attract irrelevancies that the final filing discards: see, perhaps, 'metamorphoses', below

Ahenobarbus: the nonce spelling of Enobarbus in the play. Antony greatheartedly sent his deserting subordinate's spolia after him (and so broke his heart)

resurrectionist: the doctor in the Mummers' play restores the dead to life by extracting an enormous tooth

mescalins: verb

words were longer yet: the more remotely a word is traced, the longer its grammatical impedimenta grow

we both are wrong:	which is the better medium for modern art? The raised language, imagery, and dramatic conventions of which the present halting experiment to transcend the prevailing lifeless world of cliché is an example, or to yield to this last to demonstrate our plight by abject imitation, minimally in all respects? or something of the kind

No Numbers Please

glistening hairs:	in G.M. Hopkins's eponymous poem
Bryan Pearce:	fine Cornish artist
beech or ash:	silky stems and beautiful scars
violation:	the (supposed) reason for the decimation
waste fertility:	Comus
Daniel Lambert's embonpoint:	the counterpart to Tom Thumb was too heavy to stand up
condemned:	the huge documentary file demanding the felling of the tree condemns the compilers to the same fate
antimatter:	matter is impossible without its invisible doppelganger

Absalom My Son Absalom

Cyclopean:	giant prehistoric masonry
Roman trees:	were masculine, but adjectivally feminine, in declension
glacier:	of which the action humanises the landscape

Fertility. . . Peru:	Is your prolixity destructive, as overcrowding is in poultry and people, or does it benefit, like hair, from being cut, as seems everywhere recognised? China to Peru: Samuel Johnson's term for the world
hers:	the proprietor ("she," above)
Maggie's:	Maggie Tulliver (The Mill on the Floss) had unruly black hair, which she sheared off only for it to become a feature of her later beauty
dome . . . left:	circular symmetry is changed by the culling into a high-shouldered list which has an awkward Japanese beauty
British:	the only English contribution to medieval architecture was the perpendicular
pro and con:	contrasting attitudes to the demolition

Final demand

Eagre:	a spectacular tidal wave up the Severn
Rackham:	an art nouveau illustrator of the weird and sinister
weights:	a pyramid of scales weights
Paxtons:	father and son architects of the Crystal Palace dome
men of war:	among other things, a long-tentacled jellyfish

Towards Amends

demi- . . . early:	created as universal servants but only half tame

Willow Pattern

David Jones: his surrounds sometimes lead in a protecting cone to the desired figure at its heart

chalk giant: the Cerne Abbot fertility figure cut into the hillside

lessening oars: Ulysses' crew diminished with every misadventure

Tom . . . free: Jim, like Ulysses, hardly made it to home and freedom, no thanks to Tom Sawyer's perverse ingenuity

oracularously: as the form of this word came to me in dream I dare not meddle with it. H.G. Wells's Mr. Polly would love it

Lily Briscoe's vision: in <u>To the Lighthouse</u> (V. Woolf) the apparition of the creative centre of the novel (Mrs. Ramsay) appears at the very spot needed for the artist to give her painting its unity